THE BELIEVERS

William James • Napoleon • Jack London
Charlemagne • General George S. Patton
Rudyard Kipling • Richard Wagner • Plato
Edgar Cayce • Emily Dickinson • Lloyd George
Goethe • Salvador Dali • Gustav Mahler
Frederick the Great • Walt Whitman
Madame Blavatsky • Victor Hugo
Norman Vincent Peale

AND MANY, MANY OTHERS.

After reading this extraordinary, fully documented examination of all sides of the question of reincarnation, you too may well join the countless greats and near-greats of the past and present who believe there is far more to life than death.

REINCARNATION

for the millions

by SUSY SMITH

A DELL BOOK

Contents

REINCARNATION
for the millions

CHAPTER ONE

The Search for Immortality

Confucius say: "Bemoan not the departed with excessive grief. The dead are devoted and faithful friends; they are ever associated with us."

For the past twelve years my life has been dedicated to trying to learn whether or not this is true. I began my search as an agnostic who had nothing whatever to sustain me when life became so rough that I was crying out for help, with nowhere to turn. I had to find a God, answers to life's questions, some sense of belonging in this vast universe—yet there was no description of God which made enough sense to me that I could accept it.

Even as I thought of myself as an agnostic, I behaved like a fairly good Christian—for I took the Ten Commandments and the Sermon on the Mount very seriously. But I have never been able to accept orthodox fundamentalism. A return to earth on some future Judgment Day in a worn-out and long-buried body had no appeal for me. Neither did any form of Heaven or Hell which would give me no opportunity to make recompense for my errors or to learn and grow and expand in wisdom and spiritual joy. And yet the idea of complete oblivion after death frightened me. When I accidentally discovered psychical research, with the possibilities it offers of proving scientifically that man survives death and that there is a realistic plan for the universe and its inhabitants, I approached it warily, attempting always to be objective and critical about my own psychic experiences as well as those of others about whom I heard and read.

For years now I have concentrated all my efforts on studying, researching, and writing in this challenging field. I am now ready to admit that I have become convinced that there is evidence for spirit survival. My admission of conviction may take me out of the company of some scientists, but it has brought me peace and happiness such as I have never known before, and I wish to share this with others. I really do not care which approach to immortality the reader chooses—I only wish he could catch my enthusiasm for some kind of a belief in life after death.

Does man live after death? Why are most of us actually so reluctant to mention it? F. W. H. Myers in his classic *Human Personality and its Survival of Bodily Death* says that it is the greatest paradox of life that man has spent so little time investigating scientifically the question which should be most important of all to him—what happens to him when he dies. Even if we were going to make a trip abroad we would show more interest.

Deeply religious Christians accept on faith that they will survive death in some form, and they are content not to wonder how or where, except as they glean it from their interpretations of Biblical statements. They are told they must not try to "rend the veil" and so they don't. Muslims, Buddhists, Zoroastrians, Bahais, and other religious groups who are given more detail about what to expect after death seem to be fairly relaxed about their prospects. Spiritualists and some psychical researchers believe they have evidence that they can communicate with those who have passed on, and they are quite placid as a result. But the majority of modern Europeans and Americans, if they allow themselves to think at all about the problem, are in rather a tizzy about the whole thing.

We can blame most of this on materialism—the doctrine that matter is the only reality and that everything in the world, including thought, will, and feeling, can be explained only in terms of matter. This has been the major

10

philosophical concept in the West for so long that many of us were raised with a complete inability to consider the possibility that we have a "soul," or any element within us which could survive death. But now, materialism has been exposed as a fraud by modern physics research, which, in exploding the atom and discovering it to contain nothing but space and a miniscule amount of force or energy, has also exploded the myth that matter is solid. As a result, we should once again be allowed to speak in polite society about the soul. Perhaps we may also be forgiven, then, for suggesting with Myers that it is important for us to learn scientifically whether or not this soul does survive death. As Raynor C. Johnson says in *Nurslings of Immortality*, "There is no greater or more responsible task facing this generation than an honest and fearless search for the truth." And not the least important is the truth about our ultimate destiny.

Even though the old are in need of this knowledge, it is much more likely to be the young people of today who will do the most about survival research, for they are the ones whose minds are open to new ideas. They have dedicated themselves to breaking out of the narrow routines of thinking which have kept their elders in ruts. I do not refer to those who are seeking instant illumination via psychedelic drugs, instant freedom in sex, and instant adulthood by throwing off all shackles. I refer to the vast majority of responsible youths who are making a worthwhile reputation for themselves as innovators. I find that many of the young people in my radio, television, and lecture audiences will listen intently when I tell them that the study of ESP, extrasensory perception—which is knowledge gained without the use of the normal senses—suggests that man has some extra-bodily factor in his makeup. They pay attention when I intimate that "out-of-body experiences" indicate that there is something in man which can function external to his body while he is living, and which could therefore logically survive it at death. They are attentive when I say that through alleged communication with the spirit world

11

there has come such evidence as to indicate that man can consciously survive death. These young people then ask me such questions as, "What is it said to be like in the spirit world?" "Have descriptions been given about how we progress after death?" and "Where can we learn more about this evidential information to which you refer?"

I always look first to science, of course, for verification. Unfortunately, with all the material available suggestive of survival evidence, science still does not have a definitive answer to the question of immortality. Our money is being spent on moon shoots and space flights which, while adding to our national prestige, do nothing to increase our mental or emotional security; but very little money is spent on survival research. Parapsychologists are the only scientists who are dealing officially with man's unknown mental abilities which might someday prove that he has within him some element which could survive death; but I find that many eminent men in other disciplines have strong personal convictions that there is life after death and that it someday will be proved scientifically. Until then, parapsychologists are justifiably dealing with their entire subject in a careful manner, not wishing ghosts and other things that go bump in the night to get in the way of their genuine academic research.

Most of the interest in life after death, therefore, centers in groups which assemble around well-known mediums, or in the followers of great psychics or occult leaders of the past. There are a number of these with world-wide memberships which are particularly active in the United States. The Theosophical Society was founded in 1875 in New York City by Madame H. P. Blavatsky, Colonel S. H. Olcott, and others. It has thousands of members throughout the world, as does the Order of Rosicrucians, an age-old brotherhood of learning. The Association for Research and Enlightenment, based on the readings given by the "Virginia Beach seer" Edgar Cayce, who died in 1945, has chapters in every major city in the country. The Swedenborgian Church is a genuine Protestant denomination inspired by the revelations of Emmanuel Swedenborg, who lived from 1688 to 1772 and who believed that he made daily pilgrimages for twenty-eight years into the spirit world.

Spiritual Frontiers Fellowship, an organization of laymen and pastors of many Protestant and Catholic churches, as well as rabbis of Jewish temples, has a wide and active membership. Its purpose is to sponsor, explore, and interpret the growing interest in psychic phenomena and mystical experiences within the church, wherever these experiences relate to effective prayer, spiritual healing, or personal survival. The Reverend Samuel S. Rizzo, Ph.D., minister of Rosedale Presbyterian Chapel, Princeton, N.J., says in *Gateway*, the journal of the Spiritual Frontiers Fellowship, "In the last analysis, the ultimate goal of all concerned is to establish the survival of the soul after death as a truth capable of empirical verification. This truth, once scientifically demonstrated, would produce such worldshaking consequences for religion and science that it would promote itself."

Persons who belong to these various organizations, and others like them, have already found a peace that to them is quite comforting. Having become convinced of personal immortality, they are sure that they will have other chances to learn and improve themselves, whether in Heaven, in other planes of existence, or in rebirth back on earth. They know they are here in order to gain wisdom which will be useful to them in the future. They try to see in each new day and in each new experience an opportunity from which they may learn to improve themselves.

Those who equate all zealous truth seekers in off-beat areas with the "cultists" performing kooky acts or spouting ridiculous statements are making a big mistake in undervalueing many true inquirers after spiritual enlightenment. These, instead, are actually warm, generous, open-minded, and charming people. They have the enthusiasm to enjoy life every moment. They are usually busily working to help others, because they believe that Christ, and Buddha, and all the great ones who told us to love our fellow men meant it. They know that it takes work and discipline actually to live according to your better precepts, but they are willing to spend the time and effort improving themselves because they are sure that it will be to their advantage later—as well as now. Whether or not their beliefs are based on scientifically proved data does not matter. What they practice makes their lives worthwhile, peaceful, and successful—now. If it also gives them a head start into the future—well and good.

All those who profess any off-beat religious or metaphysical concepts meet scorn at óne time or another if their persuasions are different from those accepted by the mass of their fellow men. Thus Spiritualists who think they communicate with the departed are laughed at by many who are miserable because *they* have no belief at all and would like to see everyone else in their same leaky boat. (I know because I was once in exactly that situation myself. I thought "believers" were frightfully naive.) Thus also did the Romans scoff at the early Christians who preferred to follow to their death the teachings of a Jewish carpenter who came back from the dead. Thus a book on the best seller list about Edgar Cayce, *The Sleeping Prophet*, is sneered at in a *Time* magazine review with the caption, "What the Public Will Buy." Yes, it's easy enough to call survivalists gullible—yet most of them have tried much harder than the scoffers to find life's answers and have finally hit upon something that makes sense to them.

There is no doubt that what most of us need is what Stewart Edward White calls "the re-establishment of the old faith in the continuity, the worthwhileness, the purpose, and the responsibility of life." In his book *The Unobstructed Universe,* in which White reports the evidence which eventually convinced him that he was communicating with his deceased wife Betty, he quotes her as saying through a medium, "It is only when people who have become stiff-necked and proud of their own self-sufficiency are forced by sorrow to take time to seek after truth—when they themselves *want* truth—that truth can comfort them or again make them free."

Betty also said, "The thing most needed by the human race is a renewal of faith in its own immortality."

CHAPTER TWO

"Don't Think of Me as Dead . . ."

Once a man has gotten it into his head that he will continue to exist after death, he has to decide which particular view of immortality has the most appeal for him. Actually, though, it is usually the other way around. One concept or another about a continued existence beyond the grave captures his fancy, and he reads what has been written about it and attends sermons or lectures on it and then decides whether or not the precepts are acceptable to him.

The majority of Christians in this country are born into their belief and accept it without thinking much about it one way or another. Many who are converted to Christianity become so because they are convinced that "He that believeth on the Son hath everlasting life and he that believeth not the Son shall not see life."

As Evangelist Billy Graham puts it, "One of the bonuses of being a Christian is the exalted hope that extends out beyond the grave into the glory of God's tomorrow . . . The Bible teaches that you have a soul. Your soul also has certain attributes such as conscience, memory, intelligence, and consciousness. Your soul is the real you. Your body soon goes to the grave but your soul lives on. The Bible teaches that the moment a Christian dies, he goes immediately into the presence of Christ. He goes home to a place the Bible calls Heaven."

A devout Christian who bore personal witness to the fact that her loved one continued to live is Catherine Marshall, widow of Peter Marshall, who had once been Chaplain of the United States Senate. One morning some time after his death, Catherine says in her book *To Live Again*, it seemed

16

that Peter spoke to her. "Catherine," he said quite clearly, "don't think of me as dead." Another time she had a vivid psychic dream in which she visited Peter in the setting where he was now living. He was working in a rose garden. She decided then that he was the same person he had been before his death, with no dramatic changes. His spiritual body gave him the same appearance as he had had in life. She rushed up to her husband in the dream and he embraced her with his old warmth and sweetness.

Even though she had these personal experiences which convinced her of the continued presence of her husband, Catherine Marshall bases her conviction on her religious belief. She says she cannot disbelieve what Christ said about immortality; if she did, then she'd have no right to credit anything else He said or did. Catherine likes to use Christ's words: "If it [immortality] were not so, would I have told you that I go to prepare a place for you?"

For Catholics, the true life is not found upon earth—it awaits only in Heaven, where the full meaning of each individual's destiny is finally resolved. Because of this the Catholic view of life is dominated by the hereafter. Only those who die in the grace of God are destined for infinite happiness, so one had best look to his morals. Enemies of God, or the guilty and unrepentant, are damned forever in Hell. But, you ask, how could a just God send a man to Hell forever? The answer is, according to churchmen, "God sends no one to Hell. Fools go there. God warns us against Hell very seriously. If He wished us to go there, the last thing He would do would be to warn us against it."

If Hell is the fate of one who has lived an evil life and died without repentance, there is more hope for other Catholics, whose lives reflect some good and perhaps a few major indiscretions. Their chance comes in Purgatory. There a soul found in the state of grace at death, but with unatoned-for sins, is cleansed of them before admission is granted to the all-pure God.

If any souls are already purified—and the church holds that there are such individuals—they do not need further atonement. At death these souls see God. Then they stay

17

around earth and pray for the rest of us while awaiting the resurrection. The soul of the mother of a family, for example, continues to intercede with God for the welfare and salvation of her children. Those who have gone before remain united with those on earth, because, enlightened by God, they see clearly all that happens in the world. Evidence for this is given by St. Teresa d'Avila, one of the great saints of the church, who was a mystic or, as psychical researchers would call her, a "psychic" or "sensitive." She had periods of wonderful enlightenment (trance states, or illumination) and on one occasion, she says, "It seemed to me that I was taken up to Heaven; and the first persons I saw there were my father and my mother."

In case you wondered, what St. Teresa did is not frowned on by her church, although practicing spirit communication probably is. As stated by Father G. C. Franco, S. J. in *Civilta Cattolica,* "In our times no one denies the real existence of spiritualistic facts, except a few who live with their feet on the earth and their brains in the moon. Spiritistic phenomena are external facts which fall within the range of the senses and can easily be observed by all, and when such facts are attested by so many well-informed and credible witnesses, it is useless, as well as foolish and ridiculous, to fight against proved evidence. The facts remain assured, even for reasonable men.

The Reverend Dr. George M. Searle, Rector of the Catholic Church of St. Paul the Apostle in New York City said, "The reality of the existence of spirits in modern spiritism is no longer an open question, even among scientific men who have examined the subject. Any one who considers the manifestation of them as mere humbug, trickery, or delusion, is simply not up to date."

I doubt if any of my readers are likely to decide to take up the Islamic religion, but if they are, let them be forewarned. The passage to Heaven is across a bridge finer than a hair and sharper than a sword. And if you haven't made the pilgrimage to Mecca before you die, don't bother trying for any of the Seven Heavens, for you're doomed as a lost soul; unless you died in battle. Then you gain immediate entrance to all the splendors of Paradise. If you die in a state of grace, however, having made the trek to Mecca, lived by the Ten Commandments—the muslims share the Old Testament with the Christians and the Jews—and generally behaved yourself, you may start your elysian expedition in Heaven One, which is Pure Silver. After this, if you continue to show improvement and do not backtrack any, you may continue on to the Second Heaven, which is Pure Gold; the Third, which is Pearl; the Fourth, which is White Gold; the Fifth, which is Silver (Sic); the Sixth, which is Ruby and Garnet; and eventually to the Seventh Heaven, which is Divine Light.

Compare these to the "planes of existence" referred to by spiritists, Spiritualists, and Evolutionary Progressionists. These were given in some detail through the Irish medium Geraldine Cummins in a communication purporting to come from F. W. H. Myers after his death. He denotes the different levels of consciousness as the Plane of Matter (earth or any other celestial body with comparable conditions); the Intermediate State (sometimes called Hades); the Plane of Illusion (Heaven, or the "Summerland" of the Spiritualists); the Plane of Color (the highest plane of existence in human form); the Plane of Flame; the Plane of White Light; and the final state—Awareness of Ultimate Reality (Communion with the Supreme).

The scheme of immortality which is the most divergent from all others is that called reincarnation, or transmigration, which holds that man's future progress is back on earth rather than in spirit planes or heavens. Some reincarnationists, however, combine the old theory of the Wheel of Life with spiritism so that after spinning a certain number of revolutions on the wheel they may then continue their progress in the spirit planes.

Reincarnation forms an important principle in the oldest surviving religion in the world—Hinduism—whose origins can be traced back to 4,000 B.C., and it is a central part of the doctrines of Brahmanism and Buddhism. It was well known in the early days of Egypt and was taught by several ancient Greek philosophers such as Empedocles and Pythag-

19

oras. Reincarnation presents the idea of a long succession of lives on earth for every soul, each life being like a day in the school of experience, teaching the individual new lessons through which he develops the capacities latent in his nature, grows in wisdom, and eventually reaches spiritual maturity. After that, he has his choice—depending upon which concept of rebirth he believes. Brahmanism allows him to unite with Brahman, the World Spirit, and thereby win salvation from the necessity of further rebirth. Buddhism has him culminating his long chain of lives at the moment when he realizes the Nirvana state—the extinction of his own ego. Most Westerners who go for this philosophy usually adapt it to their own likes and dislikes, while also tending to combine several of the Oriental concepts.

The idea of rebirth of man's soul into new bodies on earth probably evolved at the time the earth was considered to be flat, with a domed heaven over it like a tall ceiling. Naturally, within this limited area there was not likely to be room for all the souls of the dead, especially the way the population was increasing, so some place had to be discovered to dispose of them. What more logical place for them than a return right back to earth?

Now that we know the world to be but a small planet in an enormous and ever-expanding universe, does the reincarnationist decide to keep his own personality and consciousness and progress into spirit planes? Not so you could notice; but the theory has been modernized a bit at that. He may now be reborn on other planets if he chooses. Continual rebirth is still destiny until he achieves freedom and enlightenment by the realization of his own true nature.

CHAPTER THREE

The Appeal of Reincarnation

The charm and romantic appeal of reincarnation make it easy for us to understand why more and more people in the West are coming under the influence of this ancient concept. The opportunity to meet fresh challenges in new lives after death is gratefully received by many who are appalled by the cut and dried Christian doctrine of Heaven if you've been good on earth and have accepted Christ as your saviour, Hell if you haven't; with no opportunity ever to make amends if you should change your mind hurriedly when the first shovelful of flaming coals hits you.

Reincarnation especially appeals to one's sense of fair play: it attempts to explain the grotesque incongruities of existence. We can agree with Roman statesman, orator, and philosopher Cicero, who said in his *Treatise on Glory:* "The mistakes and the sufferings of human life make me think sometimes that those ancient seers, or interpreters of the secrets of heaven and the counsels of the Divine Mind, had some glimpses of the truth when they said that men were born in order to suffer the penalty for some sins committed in a former life."

Reincarnation is a concept of evolution based on the laws of cause and effect. The reason one now has so much suffering and misery in his life is because he lived so badly and performed so poorly in previous incarnations. During your time between your last death and your present birth you have chosen the situation in which you now find yourself, so as to make amends. Therefore, as you spin around on the Wheel of Life you may sometimes be rich and sometimes poor, changing from time to time in sex and in race. Many who believe in reincarnation think that every possible type of experience which can occur to anyone on earth must occur to all, at one time or another. And you have plenty of time for it, although it varies depending on which particular concept appeals to you. The Wheel of Life, if you're a Hindu, has thousands to hundreds of thousands of turns for you. Most in the occident, having more faith in their ability to learn, conceive themselves as able to get by with considerably less spinning on the wheel. Some here hold out for a few hundred lifetimes, and some have it down to a dozen, or even to only three or four.

The vast differences in personal potential are explained by rebirth. If you were particularly bright in music in a past life, you may be a piano prodigy this time around. If you were simply awful in olden days, like maybe sending Christians to the lions, or putting out somebody's eyes, or misbehaving badly in any way, you may find yourself now a poverty-stricken derelict, or a cripple, or a moron, or blind.

It is usually accepted that whether a soul gains or loses in his different lives depends upon the uses to which he puts his talents and his intelligence and the motives with which he operates. Certain personality traits, attitudes, and behavior patterns are thought by some to persist in succeeding lives—while others will tell you that there's no such thing. Still, all will agree with Gina Cerminara, author of several books on this subject, that the many lives, both in the past and in the future, are like chapters in a long story of growth and evolution, all of them governed by cosmic laws as precise as those which govern the chemistry and physics of matter.

Reincarnation operates around the unfoldment of a law of life which in Hindu is called Karma, a Sanskrit word meaning action and reaction, or cause and effect. The Christians say it, "As ye sow, so shall ye reap; as ye do unto others, so shall it be done unto you." But where the Christians conceive of their cause and effect as taking place during one earth life, and the Evolutionary Progressionists say it starts on earth and then continues into spirit planes of existence, reincarnationists carry it over from one earth life to another. According to the law of Karma a person is born in any lifetime in exactly the set of circumstances and with exactly the hereditary endowments appropriate to the merits and demerits of character he has established in previous lifetimes. To Gina Cerminara this is fair and just. She says in *Many Lives, Many Loves,* that the well-meaning soul who unintentionally blunders and creates problems in another man's life will not be sent to everlasting torment. He will be returned to earth perhaps to become the victim of someone else's stupid mistakes. Thus he may gain some insight into common sense behavior.

Helena P. Blavatsky, who instilled the Wheel of Life into her Theosophical Society, says in her book *The Secret Doctrine,* "Those who believe in *Karma* have to believe in *Destiny,* which, from birth to death, every man is weaving thread by thread around himself, as a spider does his cobweb; and this Destiny is guided either by the heavenly voice of the invisible *prototype* outside of us, or by our more intimate *astral,* or inner man, who is but too often the evil genius of the embodied entity called man. Both these lead on the outward man, but one of them must prevail; and from the very beginning of the invisible affray the stern and implacable Law of Compensation steps in and takes its course, faithfully following the fluctuations. When the last strand is woven, and man is seemingly enwrapped in the network of his own doing, he finds himself completely under the empire of this *self-made* Destiny. It then either fixes him like the inert shell against the immovable rock, or carries him away like a feather in a whirlwind raised by his own actions, and this is—KARMA."

Mme. Blavatsky believes that it is only the knowledge of the constant rebirths of one and the same individuality throughout the life-cycle that can explain the mysterious problem of Good and Evil and reconcile man to the terrible and *apparent* injustice of life. "Nothing but such certainty," she says, "can quiet our revolted sense of justice. For, when one unacquainted with the noble doctrine looks around him, and observes the inequalities of birth and fortune, of intellect and capacities; when one sees honor paid fools and profligates, on whom fortune has heaped her favors by mere privilege of birth, and their nearest neighbor, with all his intellect and noble virtues—far more deserving in every way—perishing of want and for lack of sympathy; when one sees all this and has to turn away, helpless to relieve the undeserved suffering, one's ears ringing and heart aching with the cries of pain around him—that blessed knowledge of Karma alone prevents him from cursing life and man, as well as their supposed Creator . . ."

Such problems bother Gina Cerminara, too. In *Many Mansions,* she asks what attitudes we should take toward afflicted persons, knowing that these afflictions were caused by improper behavior. Should we, Miss Cerminara asks, assume that the sufferings of others are karmic justice and thus not to be sympathized with?

These are really big questions, and Gina says that they must not be answered hastily or sentimentally. She points out that a vicious murderer will not learn a needed lesson if shortsighted sentimentalists decide that he ought to be paroled after six months of prison. The assignments of the school day cannot be covered if an overindulgent teacher dismisses school every day three hours early. A child cannot be taught obedience if the fond mother consistently moderates the just penalties laid on him by the father. If you believe in reincarnation you believe that "the restraints put upon man in the form of disfigurements and misfortune represent in reality the educative intentions of the universe. How, then, can we dare interfere with the operation of a cosmic law?"

If we see, living in the degradation of unspeakable poverty, the contorted, pitiful victim of a terrible disease, we cannot help feeling a surge of pity for him, Miss Cerminara observes. "But if we accept the karmic view of things, we can look upon that sufferer in another light." Perhaps he had been (as Edgar Cayce revealed in a life reading about the particular individual in question) a Czarist prince, arrogant and cruel, who caused peasants to starve and sent men to frostbite and famine in Siberian wastes. If so, we

24

would naturally feel that he should get his just deserts—and in this cripple he may be doing so. Can we still feel the same unreserved sympathy for this man? Can we still wish to offer assistance and comfort?

The masses of India have decided the question in favor of noninterference with justice. It is this which accounts in large part for the seeming indifference with which Indians regard the afflicted, and the exclusiveness with which they treat their outcasts. The lower caste there, the untouchables, must be working off the arrogance and evil of a former incarnation, therefore karma is permitted to fulfill itself without interference. Although their conclusion is logical if you believe in reincarnation, it is a sad one to Gina Cerminara, who reaffirms Christ's spiritual exhortation to love and service. So how does she resolve this mental conflict? By a process of rationalization, she decided to go ahead anyway and assist the poor karmic-ridden individual. "Our effort," she says, "to help an afflicted person then—whether his affliction is physical, economic, social, or phychological—is not only an experience which we need personally in order to perfect ourselves in the virtue of life; it is also an experience which may succeed in altering the other's mental outlook, his consciousness, and thereby the course of his life."

CHAPTER FOUR

What Part of the Individual Reincarnates?

As we think about this person who keeps being reborn in different bodies we wonder just who and what he is. We know it couldn't be the Personality and Individuality we know as John Jones which repeats itself in numerous forms and sexes—so what is it then? We have our choice of explanations.

In the *Bhagavad-Gita* the Personality is called Ahankara the false I, and it is a mere reflection of Kshetrajna, the real I. The word Personality is derived from the Latin "persona," meaning mask; but behind the mask, the oriental sages taught that there was a very real spiritual entity. It is that very real spiritual entity which reincarnates, they say.

I know many enthusiasts of the rebirth theory who insist that this refers to the Consciousness—that it is Consciousness which is reborn. Since the dictionary defines Consciousness as awareness, especially of what is happening around one, and also as the totality of one's thoughts, feelings, and impressions, it is absolutely impossible for any interpretation intelligently to mean that Consciousness is reborn. In no case are enough thoughts, memories, and feelings recalled by an individual about a past life for it to have been his Consciousness which reincarnated—and I refer even to those children who have certain specific memories about another life which they claim to have lived. (More about them in the chapters on possession.)

Professor James H. Hyslop, a pillar of the American Society for Psychical Research in earlier days, and Professor of Logic and Ethics at Columbia University, said in *Borderland of Psychical Research* that it is difficult to understand what can recommend the doctrine of reincarnation to its believers because it does not satisfy the only instinct that makes survival of any kind interesting, namely the instinct to preserve the consciousness of personal identity. "A future life," he says, "must be the continuity of this consciousness or it is not a life to us at all."

Some believers say they know what they are talking about when they describe the rebirth of the "essence" of the individual. Madame Blavatsky speaks of it as the Permanent Individuality. In occult circles it is known as the Soul Memory, or that portion of the person called the Atman or the Over-Soul or the Sutratma. In more modern terminology, parapsychologists call it the Psi-component; and Professor C. D. Broad, the well-known English philosopher, terms it a "psychogenic factor."

The brilliant author Aldous Huxley thought of it as being the Soul which is reborn. There is the Vedanta cosmology, he said, over and above the Atman or spiritual self, identical with the Divine Ground, something in the nature of a soul that reincarnates in a gross or subtle body, or manifests itself in some incorporeal state. This soul is not the Personality of the defunct, but rather the particularized I—consciousness out of which a Personality arises.

Are you still with me?

Perhaps Raynor C. Johnson's explanation will help you. In *Nurslings of Immortality* Johnson defines the soul as "that individualized aspect of the Self, including . . . the Intuitive Self—and Higher Mind, all of which are regarded as immortal." Does that mean the underlying immortal soul reincarnates? And does that then have any aspects of *your* Personality or Consciousness? I mean that if John Jones is reborn into Mary Smith, is there something way down deep in Mary Smith that persists in knowing that she is John Jones? Or does it just think of itself as a Somebody, who sometimes is known as John Jones and sometimes as Mary Smith and maybe another time will be Frank Ferry—somewhere in between a man and a woman? Those who have insisted to me that they have seen them-

27

selves in past lives—when sleeping, hypnotized, or having a vision—have felt no sense of confusion.

Frankly, I wonder why not. It would seem to me that this entity which lives within all these different people at different times and attempts to assimilate all the experiences of all the varied lives would end up a pretty mixed-up kid. That idea never occurs, somehow, to those who feel that some kind of magic will make it all come out right in the end.

They may be right—for those who claim to remember past lives have none of the involved, confused feelings one would think they might. I know a woman who is sure that she lived once long ago in Egypt because she saw a vision of herself there. Today she is Mary T. of New York City. Who was she in that past life that she now can recognize herself? Was she another woman who looked just like Mary T. looks today? Or was it some Soul quality in this other person whom Mary saw in her vision with which she identified? She merely says she *saw* herself and can explain it no more than that.

Sometimes people dream a story which seems so real to them that they are convinced it is a memory of a past life. There are those who will say that to dream of another existence will help you to understand the present. If you know by a dream that you were a nun many centuries ago, this could explain your frigidity in this life. Of course, if you are now oversexed, instead, then knowing your past nun experience would help you to explain that also, because now you are cutting loose to make up for your celibate existence long ago. It's really great how it can all be understood.

Mr. Waldo B. Richards of Omaha, Nebraska, wrote to the *Forum* Magazine: that he suddenly became conscious of his previous lives, which were revealed to him just at a moment of either dying or being killed. The earliest experience he remembered took place at a time when he was eighty and a leader of a band of people who lived in the mountains not far from a Persian village. The village was surrounded by a stone wall. At the moment of passing out, he was being stoned by six or eight men who were his executioners, using stones approximately four to six inches thick. It only took one stone to do the trick. Later, he writes, he watched his followers carry his body back up to the caverns where he'd lived. There was an opening about nine feet square cut in a keystone shape that led down into the burial vault. He stood around and watched his mourners for a while, then turned and walked through the wall, perhaps fifteen to fifty feet. That was all he remembered.

After telling about other violent deaths, Mr. Richards said it takes approximately twenty to thirty years for the average living soul to encounter the invisible spirits, "and even then they do not always let you know exactly as to your past existences."

The editor of the *Forum* said in reply to this letter: "One cannot help but wonder why he [Mr. Richards] should be so sure that these memories were actually his of former lives, when he accepts the fact that they were told to him by spirits. Had he not believed in reincarnation, he would probably have been quite willing to give credit where credit is due—to spirit influence—if, indeed, it was even that."

What the *Forum* editor is referring to here is explained by Dr. C. J. Ducasse, the gracious and wise Professor Emeritus of Philosophy at Brown University, in *A Critical Examination of the Belief in a Life after Death*. Dr. Ducasse urges that we consider the possibility of mediumship. Thus, the person through whose organs of expression true statements are uttered concerning the past life on earth of a deceased person is not a reincarnation of the mind of the deceased. Instead, this person may be a *medium* through whose temporarily borrowed lips or hand the surviving discarnate mind of the deceased speaks or writes, mentioning facts of its remembered past life that are adequate to identify him.

Some mediums go into trance, and some do not. Some are "impressed" with information purporting to come from the mind of a deceased entity. There is much evidential material which has been received through many famous mediums which is indicative of spirit survival, but this is not the place to go into it. There are many books which cover it well. Oddly enough, as we will later observe, some mediums speak of reincarnation, even though the majority of them do not.

An experience which is often referred to as evidence for reincarnation is called "déjà vu" by psychologists. That means "already seen" or "seen before." An individual may have a sudden conviction that he has previously seen the same sight or lived through the same event he is now experiencing. In such cases, the person concerned sometimes credits the fact that something he is now experiencing for the first time feels familiar to him, as being evidence that he must have seen it in an earlier life. "Déjà vu," however, is just as likely to occur when you are stepping into a newly built house as it is in an old one. This makes the whole thing very confusing.

Charles Dickens describes this feeling very well in *David Copperfield:* "We have all some experience of a feeling, that comes over us occasionally, of what we are saying and doing having been said and done before, in a remote time—of our being surrounded, dim ages ago, by the same faces, objects, and circumstances—of our knowing perfectly what will be said next, as if we suddenly remembered it!"

In *Guy Mannering,* one of his first novels, Sir Walter Scott referred to the same thing: "Why is it that some scenes awaken thoughts which belong, as it were, to dreams of early and shadowy recollections, such as old Brahmin moonshine would have ascribed to a state of previous existence? How often do we find ourselves in society which we have never before met, and yet feel impressed with a mysterious and ill-defined consciousness that neither the scene nor the speakers nor the subject are entirely new; nay, feel as if we could anticipate that part of the conversation which had not yet taken place."

Harry Houdini, the escape artist and magician, carried the idea straight to reincarnation, when he said, "I firmly believe, and this belief is based on investigation, observation, and, in a measure, personal experience—that somehow, somewhere, and sometime, we return in another human form, to carry on, as it were, through another lifetime, perhaps through many succeeding lifetimes, until some strange destiny is worked out to its ultimate solution."

Yet sometimes these cases may have different explanations if we would but look for them. A Mr. L. S. Lewis told in the *London Morning Post,* November 5, 1936, about an English army officer and his wife who saw a wayside pool in the country which was so familiar to them both, although they had never been there before, that they became convinced they must have lived in that area in another life. Yet subsequently they remembered having seen in an art gallery a picture of a wayside pool which was identical with the one in question.

Another instance which might be said to indicate rebirth might also have another paranormal explanation—spirit influence. The man here says he was "impressed" with all the new information, just as a medium says she is impressed to give certain data. E. D. Walker in a book called *Reincarnation* reports an experience in Heidelberg, Germany, where, with friends, he paid his first visit to the ruined Heidelberg Castle. As Walker approached it, he became impressed with the existence of a peculiar room in an inaccessible portion of the building. A paper and pencil were provided, and Walker proceeded to draw a diagram of the room, even including its unique floor. His diagram and description were perfect, when he afterwards visited the room.

Another impression came to the man with regard to a book, which he was made to believe was in the old library of Heidelberg University. He not only knew what the book was, but even felt that a certain name of an old German professor would be found written in it. A search was made for the volume but it was not found. Still, Walker's impression persisted, and another effort was made to find the book; this time he was rewarded for his pains. "Sure enough, there on the margin of one of the leaves was the very name I had been given in such a strange manner."

A similar incident, which also was credited to reincarnation, occurred to Mrs. W. Barnard, of Cowbridge Road, Kenton, Middlesex, England. She said, "I was motoring with my husband in Ontario, Canada. As we were approaching Smith's Falls I started to describe the town. My husband knew I had never been in Canada before, so he was surprised when I described a part of the main street—a grocer's shop, name of Desjardins, on one corner, opposite a Royal Bank of Canada branch on the other corner.

"Our surprise was completed when we drove up the main street and saw the bank on one corner and a grocer's shop—that was not Desjardins. My husband stopped the car and went into the grocer's shop. There he was informed that the last owner's name was Desjardins, thirty years ago."

This is a fascinating psychic experience of Mrs. Barnard's, but if she had lived in that town and been reincarnated why would she only remember such a small incident and locality? I would rather lean toward ESP as the explanation for this. Extrasensory perception, clairvoyance, or postcognition can take care of a great many of our unexplained problems.

CHAPTER FIVE

Different Concepts of Reincarnation

Theories about reincarnation are like fingerprints—no two are alike. This is one of its charms. Indeed, it is truly a diverting philosophy because you can make up your own rules. There being no way to prove whether or not you did have a past life, you can dream, imagine, or envision all kinds of former escapades for yourself and no one can say you are not right. You can spend as much money as you like having past-life readings, and if they are colorful enough you may add interest and dimension to your life by believing them.

If you don't like the ideas other people have promoted, you can change them to suit yourself. Just because the Hindu believes he must spin around on a Wheel of Life in thousands of incarnations doesn't mean that you have to have more than five or ten lives, as *you* prefer. If you love animals and don't particularly want cats to have to turn into less elegant human beings, your theory doesn't have to include transmigration (or metempsychosis) to and from the animal kingdom. But those who can only understand the concept if all life is in evolution and progresses upward from the mineral, through plant and animal to the human, are quite free to come and go as tigers or pussycats if they wish.

If it makes you happier to think, as some do, that in every life you meet a totally new set of people, proclaim it from the housetops. You will only get argument from those who believe they are destined to interchange relationships with almost everybody they now know. Yes, there are many who hold that your husband in this life was your mother in your last life and will probably be your son, or daughter in your next life. To them such a fantastic muddle of personalities seems perfectly logical. To these people the only way to explain that sometimes unusually strong attraction (or antipathy) which we often have to others the moment we meet is because we and this other person have been lovers, or mates, or siblings, or enemies in another incarnation. It is very flattering to tell someone when you meet him that you must have been lovers in a past life. (And it doesn't exactly close doors in this life, either.)

Psychologists are more inclined to base such attractions on our personal value systems—psychological attitudes which we have built up over the years; but what has psychology to do with reincarnation?

Most of my reincarnationist friends today do not believe they have to be reborn more than five or ten times on earth. Giving themselves credit for being able to learn life's lessons at a fairly fast clip, they have only sympathy for the poor Hindu untouchables who are so apathetic because they believe themselves destined to spin around on their Wheel of Life almost interminably. While in the West it is usually taken for granted that one reincarnates as a means of improving himself and must continue until he becomes good and wise and strong of character, Yogis and Buddhists must go through thousands of lives until they learn the secret technique which will get them off the spinning wheel—how to achieve Nirvana. Or course, if they can learn this secret in one lifetime—they've got it made.

Nirvana, as described by Eugene S. Rawls in *Yoga Philosophy for Americans,* is comparable, I think, to what we call God. "It is Supreme Consciousness and is equated with the supreme being or supreme entity named the world over by different names," he says. Some of these titles for the supreme being are Universal Mind, Supreme Consciousness, Mukti, Moksha, God, Allah, Tao, Buddha-Nature, Brahma, Higher Self. In Japan, Universal Mind is called Satori. In India, it is Samadhi or Nirvana. It seems to be the goal of all good Yogis to achieve absorption into this

Universal Mind. And this, apparently, is the only way to get off that merry-go-round of numerous lives which was so unappealing to the Buddha that he called it "the vicious cycle." Yet even if most Indians know the particular techniques for getting out of the vicious cycle, they don't seem to have the knack of applying it, for they believe themselves to be caught in an eternal round of rebirths on earth. Apparently the trick of release isn't too difficult, according to Rawls, who recommends Raja Yoga, the science of mind control, as the secret.

The ultimate objective of the varying branches of Yoga, according to Rawls, is to overcome that illusory notion of having a self which is a unit unto itself, separated from and independent of the rest of the world. If the mind is thus controlled to the point of stillness, it may experience a direct insight into the nature of the source of its consciousness. When this occurs, the individual is freed from the illusion of having a separated ego-entity, he experiences God, and is consequently liberated for all time from karma and suffering.

This state in which he then finds himself is called Nirvana, and it is the only way to get out of the spinning life cycle, according to Rawls and the yogis. To them nothing but achieving Nirvana is important, for self-improvement, which we've been told is the goal of reincarnation, is not the road to Nirvana.

Rawls explains it this way: Let's assume that the individual succeeds in developing humility, true universal compassion, brotherly love, inner calm, truth telling, physical and mental purity, etc.; in short, all those characteristics identified with the immortal sages, saints, and enlightened beings of the human race. Still with me? Okay. Now we ask if the elimination of *all* imperfections and the acquisition of *all* the highest traits bring you to the realization of your real self? Will this liberate you from the wheel of karma and its suffering?

The answer is, No. Self-improvement, no matter how far you go with it, does not result in liberation from the wheel of life and suffering. It is a worldly endeavor whose purposes range from greed to therapy, from vanity to heroism, from deception to altruism.

The cure of suffering, according to Rawls, is the annihilation for all time of the *notion* of an ego-entity, a personality, a being, or a separated individuality. When this goes, so goes all the rest of the endlessly self-generating line of traits and characteristics that are the symptoms of suffering.

The state of Nirvana is enlightenment, liberation, and Universal Mind. "Universal Mind," says Rawls, "is another and a very ancient name for the reality of which we speak." Universal Mind is pure bliss and contact with it is the goal of life and of Yoga, the reason why we are here. Experiencing Universal Mind is the answer to the questions, Who am I? Why am I here? and What's it all for? The state of Universal Mind is reached when the movement of the finite mind has been controlled and stopped and the illusion of being an individual self, separated from other individual selves and from the world, has been annihilated.

And yet if the picture Rawls has given makes you think that the Nirvana state is a state of personal unawareness—and I must admit that I rather gleaned that idea—we are wrong. Rawls believes that there is no void, no madness, no blankness, no emptiness as we (thinking now with that limited frightened finite mind) might conceive. There is the flooding of the mind and being with supreme eternal consciousness. The old, logic-bound man is dead. In his place is a supreme man, enlightened and complete. The river has reached the ocean and become one with it. The dewdrop has merged into the shining sea.

Doesn't this sound great? And poetic? But it worries this logic-bound wretch that without my frightened finite little old mind to accompany me I might not know it when my dewdrop merges with the shining sea. I, Susy Smith (in a highly perfected state, of course), want to be there when it happens and know what is going on!!! Am I an ego-maniac or something?

Another reincarnationist, Allan Kardec, in *The Spirits' Book* is on quite a different kick from the Yogis. Or maybe he's on the same one but saying it differently. It's hard to tell. He says: "Those who think that the soul returns after death into the universal whole are in error if they imagine that it loses its individuality, like a drop of water that falls into the ocean; they are right if they mean by *the universal whole* the totality of incorporeal beings, of which each soul or spirit is an element."

Kardec goes on, "If the souls were blended together into a mass, they would possess only the qualities common to the totality of the mass; there would be nothing to distinguish them from one another, and they would have no special, intellectual, or moral qualities of their own. But the communications we obtain from spirits give abundant evidence of the possession by each spirit of the consciousness of the *me,* and of a distinct will, personal to itself; the infinite diversity of characteristics of all kinds presented by them as at once the consequences and the evidence of their distinctive personal individuality. If, after death, they were nothing but what is called the 'Great Whole,' absorbing all individualities, this whole would be uniform in its characteristics . . ."

As he talks about progression in spirit planes of existence we could almost think that Kardec is a Spiritualist, but no, he called his sect Spiritism and insisted that there be *no* confusion between the two. The concept of Spiritism, which came to Kardec through spirit communication, combines progress in planes after death, *and* reincarnation. If you're going to invent a new philosophy of your own, you might as well incorporate everything you can get into it. But it must be your own interpretation—not anybody else's, and so he and Madame Blavatsky were at odds too. The Madame condemned the Kardec school because of its belief in an arbitrary and immediate reincarnation. She thought, of course, that reincarnation takes place not by trying for it, but automatically at the end of many centuries spent in a blissful world called "devachan."

Kardec's reincarnation was definitely for the purpose of expiation, making amends for wrongdoing or guilt, and "progressive improvement of mankind." None of this Nir-

37

vana stuff for him. Reincarnation is a necessity imposed on men by God, "as the means of attaining perfection . . . In order to do this, it is necessary for each individual to undergo all the vicissitudes of corporeal existence."

We hardly know which of these prolific propounders to believe, do we? I personally hope they are all wrong, but I'll defend to the death their right to have their own opinions about it all.

To Kardec, his idea of reincarnation is the only way in which the justice of God can be understood; the only one which can explain the future and furnish us with a sound basis for our hopes, because it offers us the means of redeeming our errors through new trials. If his readers don't like the idea that souls have to pass through many incarnations on earth and prefer to believe differently, they really are not at liberty to do so. Why, Kardec wonders, would they suppose that God has consulted their wishes and opinions in regulating the universe? "Either the law of reincarnation exists," he says, "or it does not exist. If it exists, no matter how displeasing it may be to them, they will be compelled to submit to it; for God will not ask their permission to enforce it." In vain may you rebel against the necessity to be reborn again, like a child refusing to go to school, or a condemned criminal resisting prison. You will have to submit to your fate, no matter how unwilling you may be to do so. Kardec adds that it might not be so bad, after all, for your conditions in your next incarnation depend upon yourselves now; and by your actions in your present life you might make your next one almost endurable.

Even with Kardec's reassurances, I can see myself hanging onto the edge of the etheric, kicking and fighting like a petulant child, and absolutely refusing to come back into another body. I'll set up such a fuss as Heaven never heard, before I'll come back again and go through all the hell on earth I've had to endure this time. Oh, dear, probably just by having such naughty thoughts I'm ruining my chances for a better life experience next time round.

If just plain rebirth, without any fancy ribbons or embellishments, is difficult for me to accept, think of that appalling Eternal Return idea of German philosopher Friederich Nietzsche and others, that everything in the universe keeps repeating itself, down to the minutest detail. And yet it appealed to J. B. Priestley enough that he wrote a play called "I Have Been Here Before" which was based on the idea that the same events occur over and over again, that men find themselves, after millions of years, in situations which they had previously encountered, and that, each time, they make the same mistakes which cause the same tragedies. Priestley did try to discover a way out of this dilemma for his characters, and who can blame him?

Thank God for such sensible modern thinkers as Gina Cerminara, who has her doctor's degree in psychology from the University of Wisconsin and is a woman of experience and tolerance. While advocating reincarnation, she says, "The eternal recurrence idea, if it is regarded as a mechanical and absolutely repetitive process, is in my opinion both nightmarish and unbelievable, and can alienate those who might otherwise find the theory of the soul's return a plausible and helpful one." To Gina "reincarnation makes psychological sense only if it is seen as an evolutionary and, in a sense, spiral process." In this she agrees with Kardec, who maintains that "a spirit's successive corporeal existences are always progressive, and never retrograde; but rapidity of our progress depends on the efforts we make to arrive at perfection." Shades of Raja Yoga!!!

Where does Madame Blavatsky fit into all this? Somewhere just about in the middle, I would say. In *The Secret Doctrine* she speaks of "the fundamental identity of all Souls with the Universal Over-Soul, the latter being itself an aspect of the Unknown Root; and the obligatory pilgrimage of every Soul—a spark of the former—through the Cycle of Incarnation (or 'Necessity') in accordance with Cyclic and Karmic law, during the whole term." Fortunately, she feels that she has to explain this, and so she says, "In other words, no purely spiritual Buddhi (Divine Soul) can have an independent (conscious) existence before the spark which issued from the pure Essence of the

Universal Sixth Principle—or the Over-Soul—has (a) passed through every elemental form of the phenomenal world of that Manvantara, and (b) acquired individuality, first by natural impulse, and then by self-induced and self-devised efforts (checked by its Karma), thus ascending through all the degrees of intelligence, from the lowest to the highest Manas, from mineral and plant, up to the holiest archangel (Dhyani-Buddha). The pivotal doctrine of the Esoteric philosophy admits no privileges or special gifts in man, save those won by his own Ego through personal effort and merit throughout a long series of metempsychoses . . . and reincarnations."

One of Madame Blavatsky's followers, Geoffrey A. Baborka, clarifies her statement—for which we extend him a grateful nod—by saying: "All life came from the same great Central Source, and all life is traveling on a long evolutionary pilgrimage back to that Source. Broadly speaking, life evolves from the mineral kingdom to the plant, from the plant to the animal, from the animal to the human, and from the human to the near-divine and then the divine."

This brings up the question of metempsychosis, or the passing of the soul at death into another body, either human or animal. It was believed in the past and is believed now in India, but reincarnationists here in America throw up their hands in horror at the idea. The early church father Justin Martyr spoke of the soul inhabiting more than one human body, and he said that souls who have become unworthy to see God in human guise are joined to the bodies of wild beasts.

Charles E. Luntz, a Theosophist, says in *The Challenge of Reincarnation* that this is a fantastic and abhorrent distortion of the authentic teaching of rebirth. "That it is held by millions of unenlightened people in India and elsewhere is unfortunately true. It is a wholly irrational belief that has led to the grotesque coddling of animals, even to the point of allowing them to inconvenience and annoy human beings." Those poor Hindus who have been reincarnationists since it all began are sure wrong about a lot of things, aren't they? And so if in India you daren't kill a cow because it might be somebody's grandmother, in the West we apparently need have no such worries.

Yet the idea that you have once *been* an animal doesn't bother the Theosophists, or many others, especially those who profess to be nature lovers. The great Finnish composer Jan Sibelius said, "Millions of years ago, in my previous incarnations, I must have been related to swans or wild geese, because I can still feel that affinity." If believing he was once a bird can help a composer produce something as beautiful as "The Swan of Tuonela," permission is hereby granted.

Allan Kardec absolutely rejects the idea that the human soul can pass into an animal or vice versa. And Gina Cerminara wouldn't particularly encourage an animal to try to make it to the human state. She isn't so sure it is a step forward. In fact, writing in *Many Lives, Many Loves,* Gina says the possibility of animals becoming human saddens her somewhat. She believes that animals have perfection and grace enough on their own. The loss of these qualities in humanization seems regrettable to her, and she quotes Mark Twain to make her point. "If you cross a cat with a human, it will improve the human but deteriorate the cat."

Gina believes that the question of whether or not animals reincarnate and become human beings stands in need of much research. She says, "Theosophical material is in some instances (as with group souls) unbelievable and in some instances provocative, but in all instances unproven." Of Rosicrucian material just about the same thing can be said. If all life is evolving through the cyclic process of reincarnation or re-embodiment, which seems reasonable to Gina, then animals, logically, must reincarnate also, but, she says, "How, when, or from what to what, we do not know."

Charles E. Luntz is much more emphatic, however. Although members of the St. Louis branch of Theosophists which he leads have certain divergences in thinking from other Theosophical groups, he follows the party line all the way on this question. He writes:

"The old idea, still held by traditional religionists, that animals have no souls and perish at death is not acceptable to most believers in reincarnation. Life is life, whether in the human being, the animal, the plant, or even the mineral. Life cannot be annihilated, no matter how lowly may be the form in which it manifests. It can and does move from one form into another form, from finer matter into denser and from denser back to finer, but there is no way in which it can be extinguished for life is eternal . . . Animals (with some exceptions . . .) do not have individual souls, but are members of a species soul usually termed the group soul. This is an entity whose home is on the lowest sub-plane of the mental plane and to it are attached all the animals of that particular species. In it are stored all the experiences, or rather the essence of those experiences, of all the animals that have ever represented it on earth . . .

"The group soul of lesser creatures such as flies, mosquitoes, mice, or sparrows may have millions or billions of these small lives attached to it—in fact the number may run to astronomical figures. As differentiation of experience and environment which affects the life in these creatures causes variations in types connected with the same group soul, a severance somewhat akin to mitosis or cell division sets in. A portion of the group soul splits off and attaches the new species or variation to itself. A group soul thus tends to grow smaller as evolution progresses and variations increase. Man has greatly aided the process by his breeding experiments. The group soul is compelled by its own nature to cooperate in these and doubtless does so gladly, as its ultimate object is the evolving of the finest possible animal or other creature, fit at some aeonic date in the future to pass into the human kingdom . . .

"It is an esoteric axiom that 'all that now lives is, has been, or will be human.' The life in the mineral kingdom is on its way up to the kingdom of plant life. The latter is

42

working its way to the animal stage, and, as we have seen, the animals will one day be human."

So take your pick. It's your concept of reincarnation—make of it what you will.

CHAPTER SIX

Madame Blavatsky, the High Priestess of Modern Occultism

It is one dynamic woman—Madame Helena P. Blavatsky—who is responsible for bringing the theory of reincarnation into common knowledge in the West. In fact, Occultism, as we know it today, owes everything to her. One of the most controversial figures in history, Madame Blavatsky was either a saint or a devil, depending upon whose version of her life and times you read. Probably the real woman was a combination of the two, and certainly the more interesting because she wasn't lily white.

Huge, earthy, dirty, sloppy, chain-smoking cigarettes which she rolled herself, and not above using hashish and opium, this clever and captivating adventuress, a psychic of proved ability, had so much vitality and such great personal magnetism that she challenged the interest and commanded the loyalty of many of the intellectuals of the last century. Men and women of distinction and importance, rendered vulnerable by a passionate craving for answers to life's riddles, accepted her mishmash of oriental religion and philosophy as if it were composed of her own personal revelations. And the society which she founded remains today a strong metaphysical force throughout the world.

Madame Blavatsky is reported by legend to have come tearing out of Tibet like a tornado at one point in her career with obscure esoteric information which she put into huge and wordy books. Even though it has since been revealed that (at least in her first books) she cribbed much of her material, sometimes pages at a time, from other authors without giving credit, her followers are so loyal that they discount criticism of her methods and manners, ignore her most sordid scandals, and cling to the doctrines she propounded. Perhaps there is something to these doctrines, after all, if they have such ardent adherents.

Oddly enough, although it is now a basic tenet of the Theosophical Society, reincarnation was an afterthought with Madame Blavatsky. Her first book *Isis Unveiled* dismissed the subject almost contemptuously. In it she stated that reincarnation was not a rule in nature but "an exception like the teratological phenomenon of a two-headed infant." In later books it is an accepted fact of life.

If taxed with her change of philosophy in this matter, Madame could easily have claimed that she had merely learned the truth of reincarnation after she went to India to live, except for the fact that by then she was already insisting that her inspiration had come from her mahatmas, whom she had known from her youth. These were the alleged members of a great Tibetan Brotherhood who were said to be her constant, invisible, sources of inspiration. She claimed to have visited them in Tibet and learned their great secrets of life—before she wrote *Isis Unveiled*. And if she had been getting her information from these all-knowing master teachers, how did they come to change their tune about rebirth? It is probably in the area of her handling of reincarnation alone that the fallacy of the whole masters concept can be most successfully challenged.

Helena Petrovna Hahn was born in the Russian Ukraine August 12, 1831, of a wealthy and titled family. From childhood she was unusually bright, lively, and highly gifted. She was also neurotic, walked and talked in her sleep, displayed morbid tendencies, loved the weird and fantastic, told spooky tales to her playmates, moved in a world of unseen spirits, and was self-conscious and self-centered. She rode and hunted like a boy; and foremost of all, according to her aunt, was "her craving for independence and freedom of action—a craving that no one could control!"

When she was seventeen she married General Nicephore Blavatsky, a man considerably older than she, and lived with him for three months; then she ran away. For the next ten years she dropped out of sight intermittently; but from accounts by members of her family she apparently did a great deal of traveling in the Near East, lived a Bohemian life with a man named Agardi Metrovich, and gave birth to a crippled son who died after a few years. During this time she also perfected her psychic talents and learned many magical tricks from mediums and sorcerers of Egypt and Arabia. From then on she was always closely associated with spiritualism and mediums, even though she occasionally attempted to discredit them.

Although she grew fat before she was thirty, Helena had two claims to beauty: fathomless azure eyes of unusual size and inscrutability and shapely hands with long, exquisite fingers which endlessly rolled cigarettes, as she nervously smoked them one after another, long before the days when they were fashionable. She also had a rollicking sense of humor, an abominable temper, and little self-control. She usually wore wrappers or dressing gowns covered with grease spots, cigarette holes, and ink.

In late 1874 she met Colonel Henry Steel Olcott at a spiritualist seance in America and recognized in him an instinct for publicity and promoting which she needed to latch onto. With him she attempted to found some kind of an esoteric organization or miracle club, and by September, 1875, the Theosophical Society had come into being. As Olcott kept this organization going, she sat down to devote all of her time the next two years to the writing of *Isis Unveiled*. Not long after its publication, she and Olcott, leaving his wife and children behind forever, sailed for India. There, after many vicissitudes, they were eventually able to acquire sufficient followers so that they could buy a large piece of property in Adyar, Madras, where the headquarters of the Theosophical Society still remains.

It was in India that the mahatmas came into their own. Madame had always been receiving mysterious letters from some allegedly psychic source. At first they were said to be from John King, the famous pirate of old who has appeared through so many mediums. Later several entities who claimed to belong to an Egyptian Brotherhood of Luxor wrote; but they were dismissed when the plan was completely formed in Helena's mind as to what type of personages would most impress Olcott and others. She decided on a Tibetan Brotherhood of mahatmas, not knowing how much trouble they would eventually bring her. After inventing them she had to give them a historical background. So she insisted that they had been affecting her life for many years past, and she even found it possible to declare that she had spent seven of her lost ten years in Tibet at the feet of her masters.

The two most prominent mahatmas, whose mysteriously appearing letters soon made them famous, were Koot Hoomi Lal Singh, known familiarly as K. H., and Master Morya, or Master M. Koot Hoomi was the author of the long, rambling discourses which were received with regularity. Master Morya was said by H. P. B. to be the master of her dreams, whom she had known from childhood. Other mahatmas were heard from only on rare occasions when a statement from higher authority was needed to back up some unpopular move she had made. It has been noted that in spite of the ability of these masters to read minds, they invariably advocated strongly the acceptance of any individual upon whom the massive Madame's fancy lighted at the moment. They were singularly unembarrassed by their failure to detect impostors and were quite willing to pile invectives on them when they later strayed from her camp or stated their suspicions of her.

The peculiar existence of the invisible mahatmas was said to be due to the fact that as elder brothers of mankind, "old souls," they had completed their rounds on the Wheel of Life, but instead of disappearing into Nirvana they had elected to remain on earth to help those worthy of receiving their assistance, namely H. P. B. and her Theosophists. As they sat in their human bodies on a high pinnacle of the Himalayas—because of their great knowledge, impervious to cold or bodily disintegration—their spirits could travel anywhere on earth to bring their messages; and occasionally, when Helena had a confederate she thought she could

47

trust, the mahatmas were seen in their ghostly presences. These great old souls, so wise and so talented, could perform magical feats and other wonders impossible to mere man; and so unseen bells tinkled, pianos played by invisible means, and pictures painted themselves overnight. When a tiny bell fell out of Madame's gown, or she was caught at her easel in the middle of the night, it was considered bad taste to notice it. When a letter casually dropped from the ceiling, or a vase spontaneously appeared in the cabinet known as the Shrine, no one was supposed to look for hidden strings or sliding panels. That would have been heresy.

How could these intelligent followers of hers have been taken in by all this? It is part of the secret of this fantastic woman. She had the gift of hypnotizing her followers, as well as herself, into believing the wildest inventions of her fantasy. She was a bundle of contradictions, according to Gertrude Marvin Williams in *Priestess of the Occult*, and "combined a showman's instinct for popular appeal with the contemptuous arrogance of an old-school aristocrat. She was a fascinating human being."

Unfortunately for the Madame, some of her most ardent supporters got fed up from time to time and attempted to check on the reality of the mahatmas. William Woodville Rockhill, who was Secretary to the American Legation in Peking for years, explored Tibet many times and knew many lamas well. He reported that he had been informed by numerous lamas that they were surprised and amused at the story of the mahatmas, and that those who made claim of a Tibetan Brotherhood were impostors and heretics.

Years of study by scores of earnest followers of Madame Blavatsky have produced the verdict that the mahatma letters were written by H. P. B. herself. Add to this the fact that several of those who had been in her employ confessed to having secreted letters by trickery into the pockets where she had directed them, or dropped them from the ceiling by an ingenious arrangement of strings. A medium who had worked for her for years threatened blackmail, and then sold her confessions to a group of missionaries who published them gleefully. They involved Madame in a great deal of complicity and connivance.

Even more damaging to Blavatsky's reputation was the report of the Society for Psychic Research. In 1884 Richard Hodgson was sent to India to investigate the charges against her. He admitted that when he went he was prejudiced distinctly in favor of occultism and its high priestess. Yet after an intensive survey of the situation, with careful investigation into every phase of her life at Adyar, Hodgson was forced to admit that he found not one genuine phenomenon. It was all a huge fraudulent system worked out by Madame Blavatsky with the aid of her confederates and dupes. His report stated that there was "a strong presumption that all evidence of the existence of the mahatmas and their occult powers may be explained as due either to deliberate deception by H. P. B. or to hallucination and unconscious misrepresentation by witnesses." He concluded: "We regard her neither as the mouthpiece of hidden seers nor as a mere vulgar adventuress; we think she has achieved a title to permanent remembrance as one of the most accomplished, ingenious, and interesting impostors in history."

Two of the foremost handwriting experts of the day gave positive identification of the script of the masters as being the same as H. P. B.'s, although she had attempted to alter it somewhat for each alleged correspondent. A packet containing letters from all the masters, as well as some of Madame's many self-incriminating epistles—she had a fantastic need to purge herself of her sins by writing confessions for her bad acts, and many of them have been preserved for posterity—was shown to the handwriting experts. After long and arduous checking and comparing, their verdict was: "The whole of the writings contained in this packet are by the hand of Madame Blavatsky whether acknowledged to be genuine or otherwise."

Membership in the Theosophical Society was at an all-time low by then, and her disciples were involved in endless controversies. Mrs. Williams says that they "wrote treatises, tributes, sardonic confessions of disillusionment, called names, sued for libel, went crazy, committed suicide, and left behind them a dizzy stack of literature agitating the perennial question: Was she a charlatan?" While very few rallied to her defense at that time, she has since been cleared of most of the charges by modern Theosophists, who just refuse to accept them, claiming there is no foundation for them. In a biography of Helena P. Blavatsky, *An Abridgement of the Secret Doctrine*, the "Hodgson Report," published in December, 1885, is said to have been the basis for all subsequent attacks on Madame Blavatsky, as to her morals, the worthlessness of Theosophy, and even the nonexistence of the masters. And this report has been repeated with variations and additions by ill-wishers ever since. In 1963, with the "aid of hitherto unpublished documents," Mr. Adlai Waterman, in his *Obituary: The "Hodgson Report" on Madame Blavatsky*, published by the Theosophical Publishing House of Adyar, analyzed the whole sad story, and to any "impartial mind" destroyed it utterly.

Even though her modern followers have rallied to her defense, at the time of her expose Madame's name was quite blackened. She left India—never to return—a physical wreck, an old and unhappy woman. In Europe she raged and cursed and wrote tempestuous letters; but, never defeated, she was soon at work on the book which was to become her masterpiece, *The Secret Doctrine*. After some time spent in Germany and Belgium, where she was quite ill, she revived and went to England. Such was the force of her impulsive, brilliant character and her ability to command the loyalty of men of integrity, that she was soon living in a beautiful home, cared for by ardent Theosophists, and dominating a strong English Esoteric Section (known as E.S.) of her society. When this proved not sufficiently exclusive she organized the I.G.—Inner Group —who took double-eternal oaths of secrecy and obedience to H. P. B. She was now riding higher in the affection and adulation of her followers than ever before. Her salons were attended by mystics and celebrities from all over the world.

The manuscript of *The Secret Doctrine* made a pile three feet high! When the book appeared, its thirteen-hundred-page length had been chopped in half and presented in two volumes, and still its editors nearly went crazy. But it met with instant success and has been selling ever since. Blavatsky beat her critics to the draw in this book by stating: "These truths are in no sense put forward as revelation . . . for what is contained in this work is to be found scattered throughout thousands of volumes embodying the great Asiatic and early European religions, hidden under glyph and symbol, and hitherto left unnoticed because of this veil. What is now attempted is to gather the oldest of the tenets together and to make of them one harmonious and unbroken whole." The aim of the work, she said, was, in brief, "to show that Nature is not a fortuitous concurrence of atoms, and to assign to man his rightful place in the scheme of the Universe . . ."

One can hardly take issue with such goals. Nor, for that matter, can the objects of the Theosophical Society be questioned. They are:

1. To form a nucleus of the Universal Brotherhood of Humanity, without distinction of race, creed, sex, caste or color.

2. To encourage the study of comparative religion, philosophy, and science.

3. To investigate unexplained laws of nature, and the powers latent in man.

If Theosophists choose still to believe in the existence and power of their mahatmas, that is their business. It has also become the business of many spiritualist and "New Age" churches throughout the country. It is a rare Sunday when either Master Koot Hoomi or Master Morya does not address at least several services. The fact that they may be speaking at various churches at the same time does not in the least distress their listeners, who find their messages inspiring. If the mahatmas have the power to sit on a cold mountain peak in their physical bodies without freezing, and to continue to exist on earth many centuries after they rightfully should have died, and to lecture throughout the world in their spirit bodies—why couldn't they give lectures through several different sensitives at the same time? What's the problem? As long as mediums will welcome entities calling themselves Koot Hoomi or Morya and allow them to preach through them, there will be audiences avid for their words of wisdom. And if, as is usual, it is constructive advice, who cares whether the speaker is a fictitious entity, a genuine spirit masquerading under a pseudonym by which he thinks he will be more welcome, or even a fraudulent medium?

CHAPTER SEVEN

Edgar Cayce,
The Man Who Could Read Karma

Genius comes in a variety of guises. From the dashing, vital, egocentric Madame Blavatsky we turn now to a meek, quiet, lovable little man whose only claim to fame came when he was asleep. Yet Edgar Cayce's influence on the progress of metaphysical thought is equally as marked as H. P. B.'s, while his image is not marred by any character flaws and bogus hocus-pocus.

The Sleeping Prophet was born near Hopkinsville, Kentucky, in 1877, the son of an uneducated farmer. His earliest ambition was to be a preacher, and he used to give sermons to his pets and the farm animals. Edgar did not understand what was going on, and neither did his parents, but he was a medium from an early age, being able to see and converse with spirits all during his childhood. As he grew older he continued to exhibit unusual clairvoyant powers, although later he was not as conscious of the spirit help.

Cayce had only a grade school education, so he was unable to study to become a preacher; but he remained extremely religious all his life, and he read the Bible all the way through every year. He tried various jobs—clerking in a bookstore and selling insurance. Then one day when he was twenty-one he lost his voice. For a year he lived at home with his parents, unable to speak and despondent because the doctors could not cure him.

Efforts of a professional hypnotist showed that Edgar could speak when entranced, but even post-hypnotic suggestion did not help when he returned to consciousness. His friend Al Layne, a local osteopath, suggested to Cayce that he should put him to sleep by hypnosis and then get him to attempt to describe the nature of his ailment. Cayce agreed and was hypnotized again. The sleeping Cayce said, "In the normal state this body is unable to speak because of a partial paralysis of the inferior muscles of the vocal cords produced by nerve strain. This is a psychological condition producing a physical effect. It may be removed by increasing the circulation to the affected parts by suggestion while in the unconscious condition." Layne then suggested to Edgar Cayce that his circulation would increase to that area and the condition would be alleviated. As he talked Cayce's upper chest and throat began to turn pink, then rose, and then a violent red. After about twenty minutes the sleeping man said, "It's all right now. The condition is removed. Make the suggestion that the circulation return to normal and after that, the body awaken." When then awakened, Cayce spoke normally. He was cured.

It was diagnosis and suggested treatment similar to this that eventually made Edgar Cayce famous; but it was a long while before he was to decide to use this talent professionally. He worked as a photographer for years, had many vicissitudes, and much unhappiness, until he finally gave up and went into the psychic work for which he had obviously been designed. After he had cured his wife's illness, and helped many others, he was finally convinced of his unusual abilities and decided to put them to the use of mankind.

Cayce's procedures were always the same. Twice a day, after prayers, he would put himself into a hypnotic trance. Then his wife, Gertrude, or his secretary, Gladys Davis, would tell him where the "body"—the sick person he was to help—was. As he began to speak, they would write down the words he said as he mentally travelled to visit the patient, diagnosed the ailment, and prescribed treatment. He could go anywhere when he was asleep, and soon people from all over the country were writing to ask his help. After he had given his oral description of their complaints and the treatments he suggested, his secretary would type up his diagnosis and mail it to the patient. She also

54

kept a record of every word he said in trance; and all these reports are now on file in Virginia Beach, Virginia, where the Cayces finally came to rest. Also recorded are the follow-ups on the cases, in which many astounding cures were effected.

Edgar Cayce died on January 3, 1945, at the age of sixty-seven. He was survived by his wife and two sons, one of whom—Hugh Lynn, a nonaggressive, unarbitrary, gracious, and competent man—has carried on the work of the Association for Research and Enlightenment and the Edgar Cayce Foundation. The Association, usually known as the A.R.E., is a nonprofit benevolent organization that was established in 1931 to preserve, study, and present to the public the Edgar Cayce clairvoyant readings. In the library at the Association's headquarters in Virginia Beach there are on file 14,246 psychic readings which Cayce gave between 1901 and 1945; 8,976 of them being physical (or medical) readings. There are also 2,500 of what are called "life readings," 799 business, 667 dream-interpretation, 401 mental and spiritual, 24 home and marriage, and 879 miscellaneous readings. The original stenographic copies of the Cayce readings may be studied on microfilm at the Foundation, which also puts out a great deal of printed material—books, booklets, pamphlets, and magazines.

The life readings are altogether different from the physical. In them the sleeping Cayce gave information about what he said were the past lives of his patients, the names they had then, and the actions or experiences in those past lives which had caused certain features and characteristics and abilities in the present life. He also gave counseling based on what appeared to be a Christianized version of the mystery religions of ancient Egypt, Chaldea, Persia, India, Greece, and Atlantis. As Thomas Sugrue, author of *There is a River* (a wonderful book based on the Virginia Beach seer's life and works) says, Cayce's system of metaphysical thought "fits the figure of Christ into the tradition of one God for all people, and places Him in His proper place, at the apex of the philosophical structure . . ." Yet it all had a highly oriental flavor as well.

The many references made in the life readings to former appearances on earth of the individuals for whom the readings were being given were surprising to Edgar when he awoke and learned what he had said; because in his conscious existence he was a fundamentalist Christian. Eventually, after learning of the vast amount of good his sleep counseling was able to do for many people, he himself became convinced that his unconscious mind must know what it was talking about.

When entranced, Cayce never admitted to being a medium, or indicated that the information he gave came from spirit entities. He always said his unconscious mind was tapping the unconscious mind of his patients, or else getting the material from other sources which he referred to as "the Akashic Records." The readings explained that the unconscious mind retains the memory of every experience through which the individual has passed—not only from the time of birth (as psychologists believe) but also from all its previous experiences in other lives. These prebirth memories, he said, exist at a deeper level of the unconscious than those commonly carrying the memories which can be recalled at will. Under hypnosis, Cayce maintained that he was in immediate touch with the deeper unconscious levels of the minds of those for whom he was giving readings.

Cayce, in his readings, explained that the "Akashic Records" could be called the "Universal Memory of Nature" or "The Book of Life." Akasha is a Sanskrit word that refers to the fundamental electro-spiritual substance of the universe. Upon this there is supposed to remain impressed an indelible record of every sight, sound, movement, or thought since the beginning of time. It is their ability to tap this record which accounts for the clairvoyance of seers like Edgar Cayce when they give information out of the past. The Akashic records can be considered almost like a movie film of history, and the Akasha as a "huge candid camera of the cosmos," to borrow Gina Cerminara's phrase for it. It is also implied in the readings that everyone has the inherent ability to tune in to this historical record, if his consciousness is so developed. Edgar Cayce could not do it in his normal state, but under hypnosis he could.

Although the words "Akashic Records" are not used, a concept similar to this is given in *The Unobstructed Universe* by Stewart Edward White, a book which is credited as being spirit communications from White's deceased wife, Betty. There is some kind of a record of all that occurs on earth, Betty says, from another world. She claims thoughts are tangible things, which are received in time, and thus are indestructible. If one ever thinks a thought or says a word, it becomes indelible in time, and cannot be taken out. That law of indestructibility of matter goes clear through this concept.

Betty amplifies this further: In history, she claims, the facts and conditions resulting from wars and rumors of wars—any happening—remain in time, though the acts as incidents have vanished from space. The present is a condition created by events—and thought, being a tangible thing, is a happening—received in time in the past. On top of this past, we, in our present, are conditioning the future. All we think and do is received and remains in time, even though our physical bodies and acts vanish from space. Research, invention, material catastrophes like earthquakes uncontrollable by our free will, or the beneficence of a season producing harvests—all are received in space as incidents that pass. They remain to condition and influence our present and the present of all coming generations. And when psychics like Edgar Cayce dip into this time record they produce information which we call clairvoyant or supernormal.

Yet Betty White, being a nonbeliever in reincarnation, made no reference to previous lives for those on earth today as being recorded in time. Edgar Cayce did. One of the most fascinating, while disquieting, things about psychical phenomena of all kinds is how they vary from person to person, while still maintaining an undercurrent of similarity which causes them to be believable.

A sample of a typical Edgar Cayce life reading is discussed in *The Searchlight,* published at the A.R.E. in June, 1959. Its special value, according to its author, Margaret H. Gammon, is that the reading was done in 1939, when its protagonist, a young man she calls Joe, was twenty-four years old. It has been possible to check the original against Joe's experiences during the twenty years since the reading.

Mrs. Gammon began her story with the statement that there are many instances of life readings in the A.R.E. files in which people who had them found a reliable guide, a source of inspiration, and a light along the path of coming to "know thyself." In addition, warnings were often given of situations which later came true. Some of all this is said to be found in Joe's life reading.

Mr. Cayce had not met Joe before the reading and did not know of him; but the background we need for him is that he was talented in mechanical work, doing his best but dissatisfied with his job of automobile repairing, and extremely interested in airplanes. Joe's big problems were: how he was to get into such work—where to apply, whether to the armed services or to an airplane manufacturing company such as Curtis or Glen L. Martin. He had no contacts or influence, and no special training or schooling. He had had one disillusioning love affair when the girl had married someone else.

Edgar Cayce said, when entranced, "Yes, we have the entity and those records of same here. They are rather unusual. For these will need the analyzing of self, even from the choices that we would choose here, in making this experience a helpful one in the present sojourn of the entity."

Cayce then speaks of frustrations and problems in choosing which course to take. If Joe applies himself in a definite direction, "these will bring opportunities not only for a gratifying or satisfying activity, but for material, mental, and spiritual development for the entity." There had been periods when he apparently was blocked, and had associations with individuals "and circumstances that would have changed or do change the whole course of events for the entity." (Mrs. Gammon feels that this referred to his disappointments in love and also his problems connected with his vocation.)

Cayce stated that these influences all come from activities that have brought Libra, the sign of the Balance, into force in such a manner that it might be said of Joe, that a path had been cut out for him. "The gods have directed that ye will have the opportunity to show forth thy worth."

Then warnings came to beware of burns about the face and hands. He was told that there would be protecting influences. (Actually, within three months of the reading, Joe was working with his head and shoulders under a car. Just after he crawled out to get a tool, the car exploded and burned. Had he not been "influenced" to leave, he would have been badly burned about the face and hands.)

In the part where past life influences are suggested, Cayce advised a greater advancement toward a spiritual, a material, and a mental gain or development.

Before the present incarnation, Cayce said, Joe was in the United States during times of activities in the north, or northwestern land, "when many of those about Fort Dearborn came back into the Virginian land—and into those portions of same that were in the edge of the foothills."

There Joe was active in aiding the defense of his country and also in training others in this manner of activity. "As a teacher of youth, as a director of customs was the entity." (Joe is particularly skillful in handling youth.) His name at that time was Horace Cline.

Before that, Joe was living in the land now known as the Promised Land, during the times when there was the choosing of those who were to be the representatives of the Roman government. Joe was then stationed in what might be called the port of entry in the land—a native of Caesarea. He was not a collector of customs then, but rather a director of those who collected customs. He was under the supervision of the Roman government. Joe was liked and disliked by the people of his own land. In spite of his activities as a centurion, Joe became active in the service of the followers of Christ, and ultimately *gained*, through his ability to apply the tenets and truths of "As ye would that men should do to you, do ye so to them." Joe's name then was Philon.

Before that time, Joe was active in the Palestine land during those periods when judges arose in Israel. He was associated with the only one of those judges who was a woman. Hence women have played and will always play an important part in the experiences of his life; and he will be directed by many.

Before that, Joe lived on Atlantis "when there was the breaking-up of the land and . . . the journeying of those to the various lands . . . we find the entity first coming into what was called the Mayan land, or what is now Yucatan." Joe was the first—*in that period of experience*—to cross the waters in the plane or air machine of that period. Hence we find such will become a part of his present experience. *To go abroad,* to be in many lands, is innately within his experience, and, Cayce predicted, it may come about in this particular sojourn, *provided the entity stays on the ground* rather than in the air. It [Joe] will be associated with activities having to do with airplanes, but with the *mechanical,* not the *operative* aspects.

Taking the advice of the readings to get into the mechanical end of the airplane business, Joe applied at the Glen L. Martin plant, but he finally tried to get into actual flying. One day while working on a plane, he prevented an accident to a comrade and in so doing injured himself seriously. He was operated on and recovered, but was then ineligible for military service.

After his marriage in 1943, Joe was restless in his work in Baltimore and felt frustrated at lack of advancement. He disliked technical and office work. An opportunity to go into construction engineering arose, and he took it and moved into the foothills of Virginia. He has been very successful in this work with the material hands and literally works on the ground—with the earth.

While to Mrs. Gammon this reading gave Joe very successful assistance, the reader cannot help but wonder what its real value could be. Surely more effective than this sort of thing was what Harmon Bro, a psychical researcher, calls Cayce's psychological counseling. Although only a small part of his activities in comparison with his better known medical diagnosing and his life readings, it was highly successful, according to Dr. Bro. In *Fate* Magazine, Bro says Cayce's psychotherapy was good even by modern standards, being the most striking use of ESP counseling he has ever seen. When in his trance, Dr. Bro says, Cayce "handled touchy matters in the personality makeup of his clients with admirable boldness and tact" even though he was in Virginia Beach and his clients might be in Denver or Boston or Key West. Bro says, "As he lay quietly on his couch twice a day Cayce spoke for forty-five minutes to an hour about one client after another with a speed and accuracy that staggered me when I investigated several hundred of his cases."

Now, if Edgar Cayce's psychological counseling was this good, and his medical diagnoses as accurate as we know they were, why should not his advocacy of reincarnation also have been correct? Is there a difference in the caliber of the material which came to Cayce when he was giving life readings and when he was not? This might indicate that perhaps he was tapping some less authentic area of the individual's subconscious mind at those times—perhaps the role-playing part which so often puts on performances for hypnotists. Although no communicating spirit was ever stated to be speaking through him when he was in trance, that always has to be considered as a possibility, too; for we really have no genuinely authentic explanation for his great clairvoyant powers. If such was the case, could a different entity have been speaking during life readings—one who believed in reincarnation? Is it possible that the stories of past lives were given as a kind of hypothetical background illustrative material in order to explain certain facets of the personality Cayce did not know how otherwise to analyze?

Certainly, however, nothing could be more cold-turkey explicit than the following: An epileptic boy of eleven, the son of an impoverished woman who had been abandoned by her husband, was said by Cayce to be expiating the sins

61

of a former life when he had lived in Salem, Massachusetts. (According to the readings, epilepsy is frequently the karmic result of sexual excesses in a past life.) In the case of this boy a misuse of authority was also an important element in the situation, because in the days of the Salem witchcraft trials he was in a position of authority and was largely responsible for the persecution of the women suspected of being witches. This ogre also took advantage of those imprisoned women for the gratification of his own sexual appetites.

Those who do not consider the concept of reincarnation to be reasonable have a great deal to say about such cases. How could anyone believe that justice is illustrated here? What kind of a just God would punish an individual for a crime committed centuries before—most especially when he does not consciously know for what he is being punished? It is not enough to say that the entity chose this as expiation for himself and that somewhere deep down in his unconscious he knows what he did in other lives for which he is now attempting to make recompense. Still, the poor little boy with epilepsy does not consciously know that he had chosen such a punishment for his own past mistakes, and he has no memory of them to convince him.

If a child has been naughty, his father spanks him immediately, or punishes him in some other way commensurate with the crime. He does not sadistically cause him great anguish a year in the future after he has forgotten all the details of his original act. To tell an individual what he has done wrong and then let him understand that he must make recompense for it is the fair way to chastise him. Blindly to inflict severe punishment on him in a later life, when he does not know for what he is suffering, is sadistic and intolerable.

Another point apparently never taken into consideration is the psychological background which would make an individual commit such crimes in the first place. Perhaps the mother of the man in Salem had so tortured him in his childhood that he had an instinctive hatred for all women —as some of our sexual psychopaths today reveal. Perhaps also his religious convictions made him unable to realize what crimes he was committing against humanity when he burned witches. Cotton Mather, for instance, was so religiously bigoted that he firmly believed all he did to punish those he thought to be bewitched was God's will. Can a man be quite as severely charged with a crime he does in the complete conviction that he is doing good? Of course, he was terribly guilty—but is it just retribution blindly to suffer epilepsy as a child three centuries removed from his crimes?

Would not a more equitable punishment occur shortly after his death? In the spirit world more advanced entities would point out his sins to him and explain to him how to make deliberate and conscious expiation for them. He would then have to hunt up all those whom he had killed and give all his time and effort to helping them. To secure release from Hell, the doomed individual would also by his thoughts have to assist the families of his victims still on earth, making himself an invisible guardian of them and doing everything in his power to assist them with his constructive thinking and efforts. By the time he had spent generations with all those whom he had harmed, or their families, attempting in every way to help them with his thoughts, he would understand the true meaning of making recompense. He would also be a new man, and one ready to begin his progression to higher things. This, however, is getting us into Evolutionary Progression and Swedenborgianism, the investigation of which must come in its proper sequence in subsequent chapters.

CHAPTER EIGHT

Allan Kardec, the Man
Who Worked with Spirits

In 1957 the Brazilian government issued a stamp bearing the portrait of a round-faced, goateed, balding little man accompanied by the legend: "Brazil . . . 1957 . . . First Centenary of Organized Spiritism." Isn't this curious? An obscure Frenchman born in 1804 is honored halfway across the world a century and a half later—and for spiritism, of all things! Oddly enough, Allan Kardec's books, which incorporated the reincarnation concept with spiritualism, are right now one of the dominating emotional forces in Brazil, affecting the life and thought of a substantial part of the entire population of 85 million people.

Léon Denizarth Hippolyte Rivail is the name by which Kardec came into the world. He was born on October 4, 1804, the son of a distinguished lawyer of Lyons, France. His mother, a remarkably beautiful, accomplished, elegant, and amiable woman, was the object of his profound and worshipping affection throughout his entire life. He was a very serious-minded child prodigy, and he acquired at an early age the habit of investigation and freedom of thought of which his later life furnished such a striking example. His entire latter years were devoted to his spiritualistic research, which was no more "in" then than it is today.

After finishing his studies, Rivail intended to devote himself to the law, but he instead renounced the bar and took up schoolteaching. And he was wealthy enough that when he decided to become a teacher he just bought himself a school—a large and flourishing educational establishment for boys. Eventually he was invited to become a member of several learned societies; and he was for several years secretary of the Phrenological Society of Paris—this at a time when people believed that the bumps on your head had special meaning. He was also interested in hypnotism when it was very young—back in the days when it was known as "magnetism."

When, in about 1850, the phenomenon of table-turning, or table-tipping, was beginning to excite the attention of Europe, Rivail was immediately captured, because he thought it gave evidence of the existence of those relationships which unite the visible and invisible worlds. As the "Translator's Preface" to his volume, *The Spirits' Book,* says: "Foreseeing the vast importance, to science and to religion, of such an extension of the field of human observation, he entered at once upon a careful investigation of the new phenomena. A friend of his had two daughters who had become what are now called 'mediums.'" They were gay, lively girls, fond of society, dancing, and amusement. They habitually received, when sitting by themselves, communications of a frivolous nature. But whenever Rivail was present the messages transmitted through these young ladies were of a very grave and serious character. This is hardly surprising, because Rivail himself was a very grave and serious man.

"In person," his biographer says, Kardec was "somewhat under middle height. Strongly built, with a large, round, massive head, well-marked features, and clear grey eyes; he looked more like a German than a Frenchman. Energetic and persevering, but of a temperament that was calm, cautious, and unimaginative almost to coldness, incredulous by nature and by education, a close, logical reasoner, and eminently practical in thought and deed, he was equally free from mysticism and from enthusiasm." He was also grave, slow of speech, unassuming in manner, yet not without a certain quiet dignity. Although his face could light up with a genial smile if he was pushed to it, he was never known to laugh in his life.

No wonder such a man was startled when the table-tipping and automatic writing of the frivolous young ladies told him the messages were expressly for him in order to enable him to fulfill an important religious mission. Nothing daunted, he immediately concocted a series of questions in relation to the various problems of human life and the universe and submitted them to the spirits through the young ladies. He then recorded their answers.

When these communications with the invisible world had been going on for nearly two years, he one day remarked to his wife, "It is a most curious thing! My conversations with the invisible intelligences have completely revolutionized my idea and convictions. The instructions thus transmitted constitute an entirely new theory of human life, duty, and destiny, that appears to me to be perfectly rational and coherent, admirably lucid and consoling, and intensely interesting. I have a great mind to publish these conversations in a book; for it seems to me that what interests me so deeply might very likely prove interesting to others."

Much to his surprise, when he told the communicating entities this, they were way ahead of him. They replied, in effect, "Oh, yes, that's what we've intended for you to do. You will call it *The Spirits' Book* (because, after all, it is all our work, you know) and you will write it under the pseudonym of Allan Kardec."

The book was duly produced and published and sold with great rapidity, not only in France but all over the Continent. Soon Allan Kardec was a much more popular fellow than Rivail ever had been, and it is he who has influenced so many people's thinking. Since he could not keep the two young ladies occupied every minute of the time, and he was eager for more material to publish in more books, Kardec began collecting any spirit communications he could find anywhere. For fifteen years he acquired an enormous mass of spirit-teaching, then enlarged *The Spirits' Book*, and compiled four other works: *The Mediums' Book; The Gospel as Explained by Spirits; Heaven and Hell;* and *Genesis.* Most of the material therein is so similar to that in Swedenborg's works that we are tantalized to know where and how the doctrine of reincarnation crept in to alter it so drastically. Clues to this are given in an article entitled "Researchers on the Historical Origin of the Reincarnation Speculations of French Spiritualists," by Alexander Aksakof, a prominent Russian psychical researcher. He investigated a medium who had been involved with Kardec's work and learned that she had to be hypnotized to go into trance, and her hypnotist was a believer. Aksakof's article ends with these words: "All that I have herein stated does not affect the question of reincarnation, considered upon its own merits, but only concerns the causes of its origin and of its propagation as spiritism."

In Kardec's spiritism it is the soul that reincarnates. He says that the word soul indicates "the immaterial and individual being which resides in us and survives the body." On quitting the physical, the soul re-enters the world of spirits from whence it came, and from which it will enter upon a new material existence, after a longer or shorter lapse of time, during which its state is that of an errant or wandering spirit.

"Spirits belong to different classes," Kardec says, "and are not equal to one another either in power, in intelligence, in knowledge, or in morality. Those of the highest order are distinguished from those below them by their superior purity and knowledge, their nearness to God, and their love of goodness; they are 'angels' or 'pure spirits.' The other classes are more and more distant from this perfection; those of the lower ranks are inclined to most of our passions, hatred, envy, jealousy, pride, etc.; they take pleasure in evil. Among them are some who are neither very good nor very bad, but are teasing and troublesome rather than malicious, are often mischievous and unreasonable, and may be classed as giddy and foolish spirits." It is such spirits as those in these latter categories that must learn by having to repeat lessons on earth, he maintains, and they have to work in the spirit world, too. "All are destined to attain perfection by passing through the different degrees of the spirit-hierarchy."

The Spirits' Book also says: "Spirits having to pass through many incarnations, it follows that we have all had many existences, and that we shall have others, more or less perfect, either upon this earth or in other worlds." (As an interesting aside Edgar Cayce says in a Life Reading ". . . an entity, when absent from the body and finding itself in one of those various realms abounding in the solar system, tries on, not an earthly form, but a pattern conforming to the elements of that particular planet or space . . ." Luntz, the Theosophist, says: "A curious notion is sometimes entertained by those who will not have earthly reincarnation at any price. It is that man is reborn on other planets. 'Why should the soul,' ask reincarnationists, 'be pushed around from planet to planet when it has still so much to learn by experiences on this one?' ")

According to the statements of the spirits who talked to Kardec, "The earth, as regards the physical and moral qualities of its inhabitants, is one of the least advanced of all the globes of our solar system. Mars is stated to be at a point even lower than that of the earth, and Jupiter to be greatly superior to the earth in every respect. The sun is not a world inhabited by corporeal beings, but is a place of meeting for the spirits of a higher order who, from thence, send out the radiations of their thought toward the other worlds of our solar system, which they govern through the instrumentality of spirits of a less elevated degree, to whom they transmit their action by the intermediary of the universal fluid. As regards its physical constitution, the sun would appear to be a focus of electricity; and all the other suns seem to be identical with ours in nature and function.

"The size of planets, and their distance from the sun, have no necessary relation with the degree of advancement of the individuals who inhabit them; for Venus is said to be more advanced than the earth, and Saturn is declared to be less advanced than Jupiter."

Kardec brings up one point that is most interesting and curious, but I must admit that it raises more questions for me than it answers. After saying that everyone must reincarnate, when he asks his spirit teachers if all spirits may be evoked, the reply is "Yes." Now, he means by "evoked" that they may be called by humans still on earth for the purposes of communication. He writes: "Spirits manifest themselves spontaneously, or in response to evocation. All spirits may be evoked; those who have animated the most obscure of mortals, as well as those of the most illustrious personages, and whatever the epoch at which they lived; those of our relatives, our friends, or our enemies; and we may obtain from them, by written or by verbal communications, counsels, information in regard to their situation beyond the grave, their thoughts in regard to us, and whatever revelations they are permitted to make to us."

The question which this quite naturally raises in my mind is how are you going to invoke a spirit who has reincarnated and is busy living another earth life? If you sent out a call for Henry VIII you might be told, "Sorry, he can't come right now, he's back on earth living another life."

Another question this raises is: if you send out a call for someone who has reincarnated several times, who would come? For instance, poet Robert Burns, famous as a toper in his day, might since his death have returned to earth as a founder of the Women's Christian Temperance Union. If you invoked him to ask for a beautiful poem, might he not instead bring you a W.C.T.U. tract against the evils of drink? It is all really very confusing, is it not?

CHAPTER NINE

More Enthusiasts of Rebirth Theory

The "pros," those willing to speak out in favor of their belief in reincarnation, will point out that the average Western mind does not readily grasp some of the metaphysical subtleties of oriental philosophy. So, they ask, why worry? Why try to understand those more difficult and seemingly inexplainable elements about reincarnation? If the concept of reincarnation answers at least some of your questions, resolves some of your doubts, and reconciles you to your fate, so much the better. Besides, you'll be in the same boat as Napoleon Bonaparte, who thought he was Charlemagne, King of the Franks and Emperor of the Holy Roman Empire. You'll join many other famous men, of today and throughout history, men who have been or who are ardent believers in a system of rebirth.

Let's look at a brief smattering of men and groups.

Orpheus, the first prophet, poet and theologian of Greece, is credited with bringing the doctrine of reincarnation across the Mediterranean from Egypt. The Orphics were followed by Pythagoras, who claimed to have the gift of remembering who he had been in his previous lives. Plato and Plutarch among the Greeks, and Cicero, Virgil, and the Emperor Julian among the Romans, all spoke of reincarnation, and famous men here and there have been speaking of it ever since.

In the thirteenth century a high spiritual teacher, having the symbolic name Christian Rosenkreuz—or Christian Rose Cross—appeared in Europe to commence the work of founding the mysterious Order of Rosicrucians, which was said to have been in existence in the East before Christ. Its object became a program to throw light upon the misunderstood Christian religion and to explain the mystery of life and being from the scientific standpoint in harmony with religion. And thus began, so Max Heindel says in *The Rosicrucian Cosmo-Conception,* "a new epoch in spiritual life of the Western World."

The Order of Rosicrucians is not merely a secret society; it is one of the Mystery Schools, and the brothers are called Hierophants of the lesser Mysteries, Custodians of the Sacred Teachings, and a Spiritual Power of great potency. Members take an oath never to reveal that they are members and to devote their lives to work for the good of mankind. Therefore the membership purports to be made up of lay brothers or pupils. But the Rosicrucian Fellowship has been formed in order to promulgate the teachings, and anyone who is not a hypnotist, professional medium, clairvoyant, palmist, or astrologer may enroll as a Preliminary Course student. The headquarters of the Fellowship is at Oceanside, California.

Even brothers of the highest order seem to fall out on occasion, and so there is another group known as The Ancient and Mystical Order Rosae Crucis whose headquarters is at San Jose, California, and whose ancient name and symbols of the Rosicrucian Order are registered and protected by the United States Patent Office exclusively in the name of AMORC, which, they state, indicates the *authentic* Rosicrucian Order.

You will learn about reincarnation from whichever of these groups you care to inquire, because, as Max Heindel says, Rosicrucians find that "the law of Rebirth, coupled with the companion law of Consequence, is the only theory that will satisfy a sense of justice, in harmony with the facts of life as we see them about us." He states the entire concept of reincarnation as conceived by the Rosicrucians to be as follows:

"The Theory of Rebirth teaches that each soul is an integral part of God, enfolding all divine possibilities as the seed enfolds the plant; that by means of repeated existences in an earthly body of gradually improving quality, the

71

latent possibilities are slowly developed into dynamic powers; that none are lost by this process, but that all mankind will ultimately attain the goal of perfection and reunion with God."

Famous poets seem especially attracted to positive thoughts on reincarnation and rebirth theories. Among the many who were willing to be counted were Alfred Tennyson, Robert Browning, Rudyard Kipling, Emily Dickinson, Lafcadio Hearn, Matthew Arnold, and Walt Whitman.

John Masefield, England's poet laureate until his death in 1967, begins his poem *A Creed:* "I held that when a person dies/His soul returns again to earth . . ."

Johann Wolfgang von Goethe, the German dramatist and poet said, "I am certain that I have been here as I am now a thousand times before, and I hope to return a thousand times."

Among authors, Sir Arthur Conan Doyle, Arnold Bennett, and Hugh Walpole were enchanted with the reincarnation doctrine. And Jack London was one of the most eloquent spokesmen we have, as his straitjacketed prisoner in *The Star Rover* gloats, "I am man born of woman. My days are few, but the stuff of me is indestructible. I have been woman born of woman. I have been a woman and borne my children. And I shall be born again. Oh, incalculable times again I shall be born; and yet the stupid dolts about me think that by stretching my neck with a rope they will make me cease."

Among statesmen who advocated rebirth was David Lloyd George, Prime Minister of England during the First World War, who said: "The conventional Heaven, with its angels perpetually singing, etc. nearly drove me mad in my youth and made me an atheist for ten years. My opinion is that we shall be reincarnated."

Frederick the Great, eighteenth century king of Prussia, said shortly before his death: "Well, I feel that soon I shall have done with my earthly life. Now, since I am convinced that nothing existing in nature can be annihilated, so I know for a certainty that, for this reason, the more noble part of me will not cease to live. Though I may not be a king in my future life, so much the better; I shall nevertheless live an active life and, on top of it, earn less ingratitude."

Representative Frances P. Bolton of Ohio says that searching for the answers "has led me to the place from which I can say with entire simplicity that I believe that you and I are part and parcel of the stream of Universal Life—as water drops are part of the Great Sea. I believe that what we call a life span is but one of an endless number of lifetimes during which, bit by bit, we shall experience all things . . ."

It is odd and interesting how diverse individuals variously interpret the goal of rebirth. Where Congresswoman Bolton and many others conceive themselves obligated to continuous reincarnation in order eventually to "experience all things," General George S. Patton, Jr., who was an ardent reincarnationist, believed that to lead men in battle was his one eternal destiny. To him this was enough of an ambition to be worth going through countless rebirths. He declared that he had once hunted for fresh mammoth, and then in other ages had died upon the plains of Troy, battled in a phalanx against Cyrus the Persian, marched with Caesar's terrible Tenth Legion, fought with the Scottish Highlanders for the rights and hopes of the House of Stuart, fell on Crecy's field in the Hundred Years' War, and took part in all the great campaigns since then.

Oddly and incongruously, Patton also believed, according to his nephew Fred Ayer, Jr., that one's ancestors are always with him. In "The Ancestral Shades of General George S. Patton," which appeared in *Fate* Magazine, Ayer quotes his uncle as saying, "They are watching you. They expect a hell of a lot out of you." There is nothing wrong in believing that your ancestors are still with you and helping you. I believe it myself. But then I don't believe in reincarnation. Patton did. How could he account for the fact that he reincarnated and his ancestors did not? Were they destined to follow his continual fighting career throughout history, always keeping an eye on him, and yet not have the opportunity for rebirth themselves?

73

Also, I must add, what possible good did Patton think he could be doing himself in all his incarnations if all he learned again and again was how to fight and kill? Perhaps he would have learned more about life if he had chosen as great men did in days of yore. Plato stated in *The Republic* that he saw the soul of Orpheus choose the life of a swan, Ajax the life of a lion, and Agamemnon that of an eagle.

Whereas Patton felt destined always to be a leader of men in battle, German poet Heinrich Heine thought reincarnation was more for leveling the great down to size. He suggested in *The North Sea,* "Who may know in what tailor now dwells the soul of a Plato; in which schoolmaster the soul of a Caesar! Who knows! Possibly the soul of Pythagoras occupies the poor candidate who failed in the examination due to his inability to prove the Pythagorean theory . . ."

Salvador Dali, the controversial Spanish artist who delights in audacious and bold statements and wears those ridiculously long handlebar mustaches, is another believer in reincarnation. He once said, "In comparison with the tremendous decadence of art today, I am the only living genius . . ." Lately Dali has been more absorbed in religious subject matter, thereby, perhaps, portraying some of his actual inner emotions. He recently said, "I am not only a mystic; I am also the reincarnation of one of the greatest of all Spanish mystics, St. John of the Cross. I can remember vividly my life as St. John, of experiencing divine union, of undergoing the dark night of the soul of which he writes with so much feeling. I can remember the monastery and I can remember many of St. John's fellow monks."

Henry Ford, the American industrialist, once said: "I adopted the theory of reincarnation when I was twenty-six . . . Religion offered nothing to the point . . . Even work could not give me complete satisfaction. Work is futile if we cannot utilize the experience we collect in one life in the next. When I discovered reincarnation it was as if I had found a universal plan. I realized that there was a chance to work out my ideas. Time was no longer limited. I was no

74

longer a slave to the hands of the clock . . . The discovery of reincarnation put my mind at ease . . ."

Musicians who opt for rebirth are not far behind the poets in number. Richard Wagner, for instance, wrote in a letter to August Roeckel in 1855: "Especially important is the doctrine of the transmigration of souls as the basis of a truly human life." And in a letter to Mathilde Wesendonck in Paris in 1860, Wagner said, "Only the profoundly conceived idea of reincarnation could give me any consolation, since that belief shows how all at last can reach complete redemption."

Composer Gustav Mahler said to his biographer Richard Specht in Hamburg in 1895: "We all return; it is this certainty that gives meaning to life, and it does not make the slightest difference whether or not ih a later incarnation we remember the former life. What counts is not the individual and his comfort, but the great aspiration to the perfect and the pure which goes on in each incarnation."

Alan Hovhannes, one of the most esoteric and talented of our modern composers, whose atonal music is a merging of Eastern and Western styles, took me straight back to the Wheel of Life when he replied to my question about his belief in immortality with the statement that to describe it would "require several thousand lifetimes." This is because, he added, "the answer is not in the brain but in the bones of billions of existences."

Besides statements from individuals who believe in rebirth, we have communications and publications from various societies and groups who have reincarnation among their precepts. The Mark-Age Meta Center in Miami, Florida, is one such organization, which is based more or less on the revelations of an attractive woman called Nada-Yolanda. Among the various beliefs of this group are survival after death in other spheres of existence, plus reincarnation, definite communication with the life on other planets, and the reality of flying saucers and Yolanda's constant contact with them.

A highly interesting theory is published in their Mark-Age InformNations pamphlet for February 22, 1964.

This is entitled "Kennedy's Soul Mission" and states, in part, that the late President John F. Kennedy is a highly evolved soul who is a worker of the "First Ray," which represents "the Power, Will, and Word of God and is the destructive Ray, concerned with elimination of error and old ways so as to make way for new spiritual building." This magazine points out once again the well-known fact that many psychics had known in advance about the probability of Kennedy's death or assassination, quoting statements from them. The report goes on to suggest that J.F.K. once before served as President of the United States—in the form of Andrew Johnson, the seventeenth chief executive of this country. J.F.K., the article says, returned to fulfill his uncompleted mission of that term, when he took over the work of Abraham Lincoln in exactly the same manner in which another Johnson has now taken over his work. As Lincoln has continued to work with his successors, so John Kennedy will work with Lincoln in the same influencing of government.

What kind of justice is that—one man getting to be president twice, when hardly anybody else ever gets to make it even once?

It was in an effort to learn how to escape all such controversial rebirths that the Buddha sat himself down under the Bodhi Tree. The son of a Himalayan chieftain, Siddhartha Gautama was raised in great wealth. At the age of twenty-nine, however, having seen and been disheartened by the wretched conditions of most of mankind, he set out to learn how to find inward peace. For six years he practiced severe asceticism, with no appreciable results; then he took his famous seat beneath the Bodhi Tree, resolved not to leave there until he had found the key to liberate man from himself.

Gautama maintained his camp there for six years, but in the process he attained Supreme Enlightenment, and became the Buddha. What eventually had been revealed to him was that the cause of all human misery lay in physical desires. It is clinging to the physical, to the delights and passions of existence, that causes rebirth. The extinction of desire frees the soul from continued earth lives and leads to Nirvana. When this state is finally attained, the cycle is over, the great man declared.

But when Gautama was asked by his disciples whether Nirvana meant total extinction or only complete unconsciousness, he refused to answer the question.

CHAPTER TEN

What Does the Bible Say about Reincarnation?

Reincarnation's burgeoning popularity today is partly the result of questions people are beginning to ask about Christianity to which they seem to find no answers. Scholastic theology certainly does little to reply to the questions of why an all-wise and all-loving God creates some of His children to enjoy all the good things of life and others to be afflicted with too many of its woes. Neither does it explain how a just God could condemn any man to everlasting punishment in hell. Christianity doesn't even tell us where man goes after death or what he does—at least not specifically; and it usually attempts to deter any efforts to learn about it by actual communication with those who have gone on.

It is through spirit communication which tells about life after death and how we make our own efforts to improve ourselves in future planes of existence that I finally acquired a philosophy which sustains me. If I had not learned about this, I am sure that I would have turned to reincarnation for solace when I began to reach for a philosophy. Certainly one must have something which is more inspiring than the "heaven if you've been good on earth and hell if you haven't" of the orthodox Christians. Some way must be given for us to make amends for our mistakes and to improve ourselves, and certainly one life is not enough to do this. That is why the concept of more lives on earth has appeal for so many.

And yet the reincarnationists who are also good Christians, and there are many of them, continually point to the Bible for confirmation of their doctrines. They say that such a statement as "He that leadeth into captivity shall go into captivity: he that killeth with the sword must be killed with the sword," Rev. 13:10, looks as if it could be refering to reincarnation.

Because the Bible was compiled over so many generations and then translated into so many languages, it is difficult to be sure exactly what it means about a great many things, and immortality is one subject about which there is a good deal of controversy as to interpretation. There were translations of the Bible from Hebrew into Greek, from Greek into classic Latin, and then into Jacobean English. Lately there have been various translations from Jacobean into modern-day English, and they are also confusing. Somewhere in all this, the original meaning of many passages has been lost, and they are in much dispute. So the reincarnationist can claim that the original intent of a passage was altogether different from the meaning which has become traditionally accepted. The individual who wishes to argue with this can point in return to places where the rebirth enthusiast puts a too literal translation on words which were meant to be accepted in a spiritual connotation. The Dead Sea Scrolls and other newly found documents are changing our definitions even more as their contents are learned. What the outcome will be is a matter of interesting conjecture. In the meantime, let us jump into the discussion with a few quotes from the reincarnationists and arguments from the rest of us.

It seems to me that there is little to be gained in haggling over Biblical phrases—one for your side, one for mine. I have usually found that almost anything can be proved by some passages from the Bible. Anyway, there is no doubt but that some Jews had heard of reincarnation in the days when Jesus was on earth. It was an old concept even then, and had been taught in Egypt and among the Greeks. Indeed, it would be very strange if the Jews did not know about it. How can we doubt that reincarnation is referred to in Matthew, 16:13? "When Jesus came into the coasts of Caesarea Philippi, he asked his disciples, saying: 'Whom do men say that I, the Son of Man, am?' " (Jesus wants to

79

know how they are characterizing him locally.) The next verse gives their reply, surely reincarnation: "And they said, 'Some say that Thou are John the Baptist; some Elias; and others, Jeremias, or one of the prophets.' "

Also when they asked him in John 9:1–3, about the blind man, the disciples probably had Karma in mind. "Master, who did sin, this man or his parents, that he was born blind?" But it is quite noticeable that Jesus denied that the man had been punished by blindness because he had sinned before birth in some other body. He replied: "Neither hath this man sinned, nor his parents. He was born blind that the works of God should be made manifest in him." In other words, that he should, although handicapped, learn to live by God's precepts of loving his fellow men, and that he should, therefore, be an example unto others.

Such indications that the disciples and others believed in reincarnation only accidentally remain in the Bible, according to believers in rebirth, because in the early centuries of Christian history many battles were waged over issues of doctrine, church councils being convened to settle disputes; and their anathemas cursed among other teachings the doctrine of the pre-existence of the soul. In "The Hidden History of Reincarnation," a pamphlet issued by the A.R.E. Press, it is stated that our orthodox versions of the Old and New Testaments date back to the sixth century, when the Emperor Justinian summoned the Fifth Ecumenical Congress of Constantinople in 553 A.D. to expunge the Platonically inspired writing of Origen, an early Church Father, who had spoken favorably on reincarnation until his death three hundred years before.

The proceedings were about as open and above board as the Reichstag Fire Trials which brought Hitler to power, and the instigators took great care to eradicate all evidence of their methods. The Pope was forbidden to attend the congress, and his denunciation of it was flouted. "It was instigated," the pamphlet says, "by the same substratum of moronic barbarians who had 'converted' to Christianity under Constantine."

And so, although we are not likely to argue with the fact that perhaps there were original references to reincarnation in the Bible, and that there may still be allusions to it, the anti-reincarnationist will nonetheless differ with the pro-reincarnationist in his interpretation of many passages. Charles E. Luntz wants a fight when he says in his *The Challenge of Reincarnation,* "Accordingly we inquire of any Bible scholar or student who insists that reincarnation is neither taught nor referred to in the scriptures how the following are to be explained if not as referring to reincarnation:" Luntz then quotes Revelation 3:12. "Him that overcometh will I make a pillar in the temple of my God, and he shall go no more out." To me this means simply that you do not have to go out of your body into death more than once. But Luntz says: "If he who overcometh (who is perfected) is to go no more out, he must have been going 'out' frequently before that stage was reached. What can the word 'out' mean except into repeated earth lives, for which the need will then have ceased?"

Mr. Luntz's quotation, whatever it means, could well be countered with Hebrews 9:27, "And as it is appointed unto men once to die, but after this the judgment . . ."

Luntz also quotes Jeremiah 1:4–5. "Then the word of the Lord came unto me saying, Before I formed thee in the womb I knew thee . . . and I ordained thee a prophet unto the nations." Luntz says, "Can this be anything but a reference to the fact that Jeremiah had earned the high privilege accorded him by his spiritual achievements in earlier lives? How could God have known him if he had no existence before he was formed physically? Why should God have chosen him unless he had merited the choice when the Bible assures us, 'There is no respect of persons with God'?"

Perhaps for those who believe in metempsychosis—that man came up through the mineral, plant, and animal path to become the first in a chain of humans—God might not have known him previously.

"In my Father's house are many mansions." John 14. "Dwell on that," says Gina Cerminara, "not for an hour, or a minute, but for a day, as you go about your work. Who is your father? What is meant by 'mansions'? And that there are many mansions in His house? What house?"

Gina says it is one's body that is the temple. Many mansions are in that body, many temples. "For the body has been again and again in the experience of the earth; they are sometimes mansions, sometimes homes, sometimes huts."

Now dwell on it again, and consider that Jesus might have meant that earth is one mansion in the great universe, the house of God. Other planets, or other spheres—all the vast area known as spirit planes of existence—are called God's mansions. In other words, God has much more to offer us than a mere series of physical existences on earth. We leave earth, instead, and go on to bigger and greater things.

A pamphlet entitled "Reincarnation," from the Swedenborgian Press, speaks of the spiritual seers of all ages who have seen the necessity for human rebirth, spiritual regeneration, and who, for lack of better language, have always described this need in terms of ordinary birth. The Bible is quoted to make the point: "Except a man be born again, he cannot see the kingdom of God." But it is argued that the quote refers to spiritual, not physical rebirth, and the Swedenborgian Press posits that this is only a grossly literal outlook which leads readers of ancient Eastern Scriptures to find therein statements in favor of reincarnation. In the *Bhagavad-Gita* there are frequent passages which describe spiritual rebirth in physical terms. Thus we read, "We have been born many times, I [Krishna] and thou, Arjuna." And again, "Those unhappy ones, who hate and are cruel . . . I cast from one reincarnation to another."

The rebirths referred to in the *Bhagavad-Gita* are spiritual, it is argued, not physical, and the language employed is figurative and needs to be interpreted in terms of the spirit, not literally. Thus, rebirth, in such scriptures, is held to be a figure of speech.

St. Paul seems to have put the whole thing clearly in a nutshell when he says in Corinthians 1:15: "Some one will ask, 'How are the dead raised? With what kind of body do they come?' You foolish man! What you sow does not come to life unless it dies. And what you sow is not the body which is to be, but a bare kernel, perhaps of wheat or of some other grain. But God gives it a body as he has chosen, and to each kind of seed its own body . . . So it is with the resurrection of the dead. What is sown is perishable, what is raised is imperishable. It is sown in dishonor, it is raised in glory. It is sown in weakness, it is raised in power. It is sown a physical body, it is raised a spiritual body. If there is a physical body, there is also a spiritual body."

Among Christian denominations there is a conflict of interpretation of St. Paul's remarks. Some consider them to mean that when the Judgment Day comes the physical body will be the one to be resurrected. To others St. Paul seems explicit in stating that the spiritual body is to be resurrected, when he says: "I tell you this, brethren: flesh and blood cannot inherit the kingdom of God, nor does the perishable inherit the imperishable.

"Lo! I tell you a mystery. We shall not all sleep, but we shall all be changed, in a moment, in the twinkling of an eye, at the last trumpet. For the trumpet will sound, and the dead will be raised imperishable, and we shall be changed. For this perishable nature must put on the imperishable, and this mortal nature must put on immortality."

CHAPTER ELEVEN

Emanuel Swedenborg,
Pipeline to the Spirit World

Having just given arguments presented by the Swedenborgian Press, it would obviously be proper now to introduce Emanuel Swedenborg himself, another of those who give eloquent testimony for a life after death. Perhaps his information is even more valuable than that of those who have transmitted spirit communications in a state of trance, or expressed their psychic impressions, because Swedenborg's testimony is based entirely upon his own personal experiences *visiting the spirit world while awake.*

If this man had been neurotic and unstable, nobody would have paid any attention to him. They would have said he was suffering from delusions and let it go at that. But Swedenborg was not neurotic or unstable; he was a man whom psychologist William James said "had the sanest and most far-reaching intellect this age has known." He was a man of whom poet Edwin Markham said, "There is no doubt that Swedenborg was one of the greatest intellects that have appeared upon the planet."

According to Elbert Hubbard, who made a career of writing about great men, "Thinking men everywhere agree that Swedenborg blessed and benefited the race, preparing the way for the thinkers and doers who should come after him."

And Helen Keller wrote, "Out of Swedenborg's evidence from beyond earth's frontier I construct a world that shall measure up to the high claims of my spirit when I quit this wonderful but imprisoning house of clay."

Emanuel Swedenborg's writings also influenced such disparate figures as Honore Balzac, Ralph Waldo Emerson, and Abraham Lincoln. The Swedenborgian Church, founded on his teachings, sometimes called the New Church or the Church of the New Jerusalem, has some 10,000 loyal followers in the United States and an estimated 120,000 throughout the world.

Emanuel was born of a religious Lutheran family in Stockholm, Sweden, in 1688, and he grew up to be a strong, healthy, handsome, and statuesque man, commanding in appearance and personality. He was graduated from the University of Upsala with honors and received his Doctor of Philosophy degree when he was twenty-one years old. He studied mathematics, mechanics, chemistry, physics, astronomy, geology, anatomy, physiology, and psychology, traversing the whole range of science and philosophy of his time not merely as a student but as an active investigator and theorist. He spoke six languages fluently and could also read Hebrew and Greek.

There's more—he was the Swedish authority on mineralogy and geology and wrote several books on mining and the working of iron and copper which were regarded as standard works by the metallurgists of his day. He was an outstanding mathematician and the first to propound the nebular hypothesis, and he also anticipated Einstein's doctrine of energy. It is little wonder that he has been called the Swedish Aristotle and is compared most often to Leonardo da Vinci in the range and breadth of his knowledge and interests. He was knighted by his queen for his achievements; and he traveled all over Europe, where he received many awards and commendations from royalty.

Emanuel Swedenborg was not a hysterical or excitable person, but singularly composed and sedate. With all his other talents, he did not have time to be a ladies' man; and perhaps that's just as well, because who knows what it would have done to his reputation. That he was actually shy with women is revealed by the fact that when he was turned down by the one girl he hoped to marry, he never asked another, and he remained unwed all his life.

Swedenborg was a man of deep though unobtrusive religious convictions, and until the age of fifty-six his religion had no unusual aspects. Of course, he had a slight tendency to produce startling information by ESP from time to time, which rather distracted his friends and confused his historians. You all undoubtedly know about how he described the leaping flames of a fire in Stockholm, when he was in Gottenberg, three hundred miles away, and how he told a lady where her deceased husband had hidden the receipt for some silver, and those other stories that are so often repeated. Perhaps less known is that at a party in 1762 he announced that the Emperor of Russia, Peter III, had just died in prison, which proved to be true; and that when the Queen of Sweden asked him to tell her the secret that her brother had revealed to her just before he died, Emanuel replied with the exact details of it and all the circumstances surrounding it. The Queen shrieked in a queenly way that no one but God and her brother could have known that. But that wasn't all that Swedenborg knew. He was able to predict in advance the exact day he would die, writing in a letter to John Wesley that he was going into the spirit world for good on March 29, 1772. And he did.

It was hardly surprising that Emanuel Swedenborg should have advanced warning of his own death, for he had been hobnobbing with spirits for twenty-eight years by then, and in their own territory, too. The spirit world, he claimed, surrounds us; but it is normally unseen because our physical bodies are not usually adapted to perceiving it, unless we are unusually psychic, as he was.

On Swedenborg's visits to these other planes or spheres, he met people whom he had known during their earthly lives, and a great number of historic personages. He associated with these familiarly, and they told him a great deal about conditions after death. He was even shown around some of the higher planes, those almost nobody reaches until they've been "over" for a long time and are quite spiritually progressed.

Now, these statements Swedenborg made about what he had seen, says John H. Spalding in *Introduction to Swedenborg's Religious Thought,* should be accepted either as true in substance, or false. If taken to be false, they must be the result of fraud, delusion, or hallucination. But "it is impossible," Spalding says, "for any candid, open-minded man to read Swedenborg's works with any attention and think him an imposter." Thus, if Swedenborg's statements were false, he must have been the victim of hallucinations. If he was deluded about his contact with the unseen world, if all his experiences were simply his own dreamings and musings thrown into apparent objectivity, then he was quite mad.

In most of his behavior Swedenborg instead always maintained every evidence of a well-balanced mind. He never pressed upon anyone his theological idiosyncracies, but was ready to talk freely about them to those who wanted to listen. He never indicated a trace of the sense of personal importance which is so characteristic of the fanatic. He showed no disposition to form a cult about himself; and the New Church, based on his teachings, was not organized until long after his death. His writings were voluminous and originally in Latin, and they are, even in translation, sometimes difficult to read; but those who have poured over them and deciphered them have usually felt well rewarded.

Incidentally, as further evidence that he hadn't lost touch with reality, about ten years before his death, when there was a great depression and panic in Sweden, some of Swedenborg's best material was written about financial matters. He was a strong advocate of stabilized currency backed by gold; and he was the originator of the idea of amortization of mortgages. All this matter-of-fact commerce was going on while he was at the same time making his daily visits with his invisible friends.

Was it the philosophy he learned from them which kept his feet so well grounded while his head was in the clouds? What was this conception which Swedenborg propounded to the consternation of his own and subsequent generations? It was that each man is a new and individual creation of God's; that he lives once on earth and then, when he dies, progresses by his own efforts in spirit planes of existence, improving himself as he goes ever onward and upward to the heights of spiritual development—which eventually after eons of time bring him to a state of consciousness worthy of associating with God.

"Whoever duly considers the subject," he wrote in *Heaven and Hell,* "can see that as the body is material it is not the body that thinks, but the soul, which is spiritual. The soul of man, upon the immortality of which many have written, is his spirit, for this is in every respect immortal." This spirit lives within the body until death releases it. After death the spirit has a body of identical appearance to its earthly prototype, but of different substance, which is just as real to the spirit as his physical body ever was. And the world of the spirit looks just as substantial as earth ever did, because everything, not only the body, has a spiritual counterpart of identical appearance.

An individual is no different mentally or spiritually the moment after death than he was the moment before; and all his faculties are intact. His surroundings vary according to his own evaluation of himself and where he deserves to be and what he expects to see. If he was spiritually enlightened at the time of death, he will be in a beautiful place— the Heavenly Kingdom.

Unfortunately, some spirits, by their own desire, are in the state of mind known as hell, because they love evil ways and do not wish to part with them. The creation of man into a mature and fully-developed soul of the highest spiritual endowments is the ultimate goal in the world of the hereafter; but this can only be accomplished through the choice and efforts of each individual. One of the uses of hell is to help people to see and overcome their faults, and they will remain in this hellish state until they decide they want to learn to improve instead. Once the decision is made, they begin their traveling upward toward true goodness.

As members of the family of God we are distinct individuals, each contributing the value of his personality to the common good. The heavenly society is harmonious, although varied, its unifying power being love of good and the desire to serve. Swedenborg maintains that the distinctive personality of each one of us is never lost by mergence in the Divine, as in the Nirvana concept. Neither is there resurrection of the body on Judgment Day, he says. After the spirit has escaped at death, the physical body is of no more use, and the liberated soul lives forever in the spiritual world. It never takes to itself another physical body. Only once are we born on earth, and afterwards we continue as spiritual beings. There is no need for us to return to earth to gain further experience and endure further discipline; all that is essential for our eternal welfare and future development is provided in the eternal abode of humanity. It is an unconscious, but compelling, demand for bodily satisfactions which makes the concept of repeated lives on earth appeal to some people, according to Swedenborgians.

"God has a supreme purpose in creation which is no less than the establishment of heavenly human society, as far as possible in this world, but in its full fruition in the eternal realm," Swedenborg said.

Helen Keller's conviction regarding immortality stemmed directly from her study of Swedenborg's works. This wonderful woman, whose blindness and deafness were not a handicap to her, but a challenge, says in her book *My Religion* that Swedenborg's revelations take the fear from death. Thanks to him, she is convinced of a larger, nobler life beyond the grave. "The child dying in his mother's arms was an intolerable thought," she says. "Now we know of the sweet, unclouded childhood which awaits him, the bright abodes where angels will teach him to speak, think creative thoughts, and do the work for which he is best fitted, where he will grow up in beauty and go forth to deeds and adventures mightier than were ever beheld upon earth. We know now that every faithful love which has been thwarted here has tenfold greater joy in store for it on the other side."

Heaven, as Swedenborg portrays it, is not a mere collection of radiant ideas, but a practical, livable world. It should never be forgotten that death is not the end of life, but only one of its most important experiences.

"As I wander through the dark, encountering difficulties," says Helen Keller, whose very existence was an inspiration to us all, "I am aware of encouraging voices that murmur from the spirit realm . . . Immured by silence and darkness, I possess the light which shall give me vision a thousand-fold when death sets me free."

In recent years the great psychologist and psychical researcher William James has been said to be communicating from the spirit world after his bodily death in order to give us the benefit of his experience. Whether or not you accept these messages as actually coming from James, it is interesting that his material verifies and amplifies that of Swedenborg and of Stewart Edward White's Betty. Here is a statement about Swedenborg's revelations; allegedly given by James in the spirit world, sent through a medium by automatic writing.

"Swedenborg was able to give a complete report of his true experiences, although they were highly colored by his ardent Christianity. Nevertheless, he saw conditions as they really are when he sojourned among his spirit friends; and his accounts are illuminating to those who will take the time to wade through them.

"No person may read his books and not realize that there is a definite system to the world and the universe, a plan which is organized at the top and extends down to all areas of every planet. It is a plan of law and order, and only our own lack of knowledge about it causes us to deny the possibility of its existence. When one is told the truth about the system, however, it has to be told in the idiom that the average man can understand; and it is frequently difficult for future generations to comprehend. Jesus told of it in the parables of his time, and it is now difficult for others always to perceive his intent, for it has been interpreted variously by those who translated it. A new prophet comes in each era and tells his own people; but the world as a whole has only bits and pieces of the truth, which it assimilates as it may. No one person has ever taught the entire truth, for each has glimpsed it as he has been able to do so. Were communication with highly developed spirits taught and accepted so that many people could be receptive to their teachings, much more would be known about the conditions after death, the wonderful system of law and order which prevails throughout the universe, and how each of us may adapt ourselves to it so as to follow the laws to our best advantage and to that of our fellow men. No one individual has ever been able to know all the secrets of the universe; but those who have glimpsed them have led lives which were an inspiration to the rest of us. And among these great seers of the truth was Emanuel Swedenborg."

CHAPTER TWELVE

Those Who Said No to Reincarnation

Stewart Edward White was a prolific writer who published altogether over forty books and innumerable articles and short stories. Most of his earlier books had been based on his own experiences camping in the United States or exploring in Africa. His wife Betty had accompanied him on many of his explorations. Then in the early 1920's she began fooling around with a ouija board just for fun, but apparently she had strong mediumistic talents and so she was soon getting messages. Then she began going into trance and giving a great deal of verbal information about conditions after death. White sat beside her while she was in the trance state and took down everything she said, which was eventually published in a series called "The Betty Books."

Betty's experiences explained and clarified information which had been given in two earlier books: *The Seven Purposes by* Margaret Cameron, and *Our Unseen Guest* by two prominent people who used the pseudonym Darby and Joan. Eventually these authors all got acquainted and became friends.

In 1939 Betty died, and shortly afterward she began to speak through Joan, of the Darby and Joan team, who had become quite a strong trance medium. Betty continued with the same kind of information she had previously given while on earth. Apparently she now lived permanently under conditions she had been able to achieve only briefly before.

Most of the accounts which have been published giving

data about life after death, such as Sir Oliver Lodge's *Raymond,* have put forth ideas which sound incredibly naive. Betty described this as "too literal a translation of a parallel." So that she would not sound what she termed "Oliver Lodgish," Betty bent over backward too far the other way, very carefully couching her statements in the most technical terminology she could use. And thereby she made it just as confusing as Edgar Cayce's statements, or most of the other trance material available. Nonetheless, *The Unobstructed Universe* and the other books which White published giving the information with which Betty provided him after her death, have gone into many editions and have given food for thought to millions of readers.

The main concept advanced in these books is as follows: Consciousness is the only reality and Consciousness is in a state of evolution. Betty says, "Of course death is much simpler than birth; it is merely a continuation. Earth is the *borning place* for the purpose of individualization." She clarifies this with: "The obstructed universe [earth] is for the purpose of birth, of the individualization of consciousness. All matter is born in your universe. Nothing is lost." She says individuality is not lost; it is all kept. It is the highest form of matter, the soul, that goes on undivided. Still, the consciousness of matter is a very low degree, and it is at the command of the consciousness of man. It is even more at the command of those in the unobstructed universe.

Betty insists that there is only one universe and that the conditions in which she found herself after death were the same as these she had been aware of before she died. "One of those things that astounds you most when you first arrive is the lack of difference," she said.

She emphasized that every law in the universe, whether we understand it or not, extends through the *entirety* of the universe. "There is no law here that is not potentially discoverable in your world, though of course there are many not yet discovered. The same law works in both aspects of the universe." The law of cause and effect is just

93

the same in the spirit world. The main difference in comparing the situation of those living on earth with those in the spirit world is that we live in the obstructed aspect of the universe, while deceased spirits live in the unobstructed. Although it is all the same universe, we are living in it as blind and deaf persons might live in our world; there is much that we can't come in contact with, or don't see or hear.

We are obstructed by matter, but the unobstructed universe is a place where there are no solids. We "bump," as Betty put it, up against a wall—it obstructs us and we have to climb over it or go around. We also bump against space—linear distance obstructs us and so does time. We say, "I haven't time to do this, or that." This means that the fixed duration of an hour or a day or a year is obstructing to us. Also, Betty says, "You bump up against motion; some rate of speed, slow or fast, is continually obstructing you. You bump up against thought, people's ideas; every day they are hindering, limiting, obstructing you." We are obstructed also because we are ourselves obstructions, as one might say, as long as we are here on earth. But the spirits, who are not bothered by our obstructions, can pass through our walls and go anywhere they wish on earth. They also can enter our minds at will.

But this consciousness that is the continuation of the individual after death—what exactly is it? Betty says, "Consciousness is the one and only reality."

Betty also mentioned that nothing that happens to an individual is as important as what that individual thinks about it. The Rosicrucians say something similar, that the purpose of life is not happiness but experience. "Sorrow and pain," they say, "are our most benevolent teachers, while the joys of life are but fleeting."

Betty went on that consciousness is in evolution, therefore it is in various degrees, and each degree has its frequency, which is a sort of magnetic energy. She explained the frequency by mentioning the electric fan. You can see the blades when the fan is still; but when it is turned on and going at a high frequency you can look right through the fan and see the wall back of it. When it is running so fast, as far as our vision is concerned it has lost its solidity. Betty says, "My co-existence with you is analogous. If the frequency were different for your human focus, you could see me. As it is, you look through me. I am not there."

And yet, of course, she is there. It is just to us that she appears to have gone. And she's there in just as solid a form—to her—as she wore on earth. She doesn't float around like a spook. She would have none of that floating business. The accusation that she was in any respect a "disembodied spirit," a "shade," or a harp-playing angel, always aroused her. "But I tell you, we're *human!* I am right here." She was most emphatic. "There is only one universe."

Each individual is put into the world to do a job; and he arrives in the spirit world best and happiest only when it is completed; after he has gathered to himself as nearly as possible his requisite of work and experience. The purpose of the "invisibles," the spirit helpers, is to restore in earth consciousness the necessity of individual effort, and the assurance that the effort will not be wasted. "The only assurance of this is a return to the belief in immortality," Betty said.

In one of his later books, *The Job of Living,* White quotes Gaelic, another invisible, as saying that we cannot understand the infinite, nevertheless we *can* postulate a few generalities. It must be inclusive; it must be all of everything—all there is, and in completion. The Infinite God is all of consciousness; and, we are told, consciousness is the one and only reality.

The aspect of the infinite in the finite is another matter. That, says Gaelic, is within our province of exploration, and within our powers of exploration either now or in the future. "Within the finite we find the infinite has voluntarily self-limited itself to the laws by which finite creation exists. What the purpose may be we cannot even begin to guess, for it is part of the infinite scheme of things. Its immediate purpose—with which we are personally concerned—would seem to be the creation and the evolution of the individual consciousness. Expansion; growth; to perfect the individual. What his job or function may be after he has been perfected is out of bounds for our thinking. It need not begin to concern us for some eons to come."

If those who communicated with Stewart Edward White were reluctant to tell our ultimate and final goal after death, the famous medium Andrew Jackson Davis was not. "There is a chain extending from man to Diety!" he said. It is a chain of men in various stages of progression. "Let it be remembered that all spirits and angels were once men; lived in physical organizations as we do, and died as we die, previous to their departure for the spirit home." Angels, he says, are the glorious individuals who, though once residents upon some earth, now tread the beautiful paths and flowering valleys of the spirit home. Just because God is so inconceivable in his greatness, so elevated, we shouldn't think that he is far removed from our spirits.

"So near is He," says Davis, who also traveled in spirit planes, "that in Him we daily and hourly 'live, move, and have our being.' We are in Him and of Him, as the body, branches, twigs, leaves, buds, blossoms, and fruit of a tree are unfolded and minutely developed from the essences and beginning principles which were originally deposited in its germ, so does the Great Germinal Essence of the Universal Tree unfold and develop the minutest branches, buds, blossoms, and organizations which perfume and adorn the Stupendous Whole."

Note the difference in style. White's Invisibles were so careful not to overpower us with their rhetoric; but earlier spirit communicators had no such hesitancy. Andrew Jackson Davis was born in 1826 in Poughkeepsie, New York. His family was so poor that he had only five months of schooling before he had to go to work as a cobbler's apprentice. But he had so much natural psychic power that he eventually became a great medium. In his normal state he knew nothing of the subjects about which he wrote and lectured, yet he eventually won an international reputation as the famous "Poughkeepsie Seer." He wrote thirty formidable volumes about his experiences traveling in spirit planes, which were so popular that they were translated into foreign languages. His books may be "an encyclopedia of the essential principles of science, philosophy, and religion, of immense value" as the jacket of a book about him called *Introduction to the Writings of Andrew Jackson Davis* states, but few students of immortality will ever find the time to read them all, or even to know where to begin among them to acquire a general idea of their usefulness. Fortunately James Lowell Moore, a personal friend of Davis, whose father and grandfather before him were also friends, has compiled some of his writings into this book mentioned above. Even it is tedious reading, but from it the reader can get Davis' picture of life after death, as he found it.

Davis had his first trip out of his body on the evening of January 1, 1843. At that time he knew nothing about clairvoyance, or hypnotism (then called magnetism). When he was put into a hypnotic trance, instead of voices speaking through him, or his subconscious mind contacting the Akashic Records, Davis found himself actually "born again" in the spirit. He says, "My thoughts were of the most peaceful character. My whole nature was expanded." First he saw an intense blackness before him, apparently extending hundreds of miles into space and enveloping the earth. Gradually, however, this passed and his perception was enlarged. The room he was in and the individuals within it were all illuminated. Each human body was glowing with many brilliant colors as he looked inside it and watched the operation of all the organs, the flow of blood in veins and arteries, even the emanations of thoughts from the brain.

After this his vision widened. "I could see the life nature, living in the atoms of the chairs, tables, etc," he said. (The great modern medium Eileen J. Garrett has similarly described seeing all the atoms which make up a chair or a plant, when she was in a similar state of expanded awareness.)

Soon he could see through everything as if it were transparent, even the walls, then the walls of the adjoining dwelling, and on into it. He could observe the furniture there as clearly as in his own house. (This, incidentally, would make it seem that he had passed into Betty's unobstructed universe, would it not?)

At this point the operator asked Davis to perform some tests to indicate whether or not he was in a supernormal condition, and he did. "After lightly securing my bodily eyes with handkerchiefs, he placed some books on a horizontal line with my forehead, and I saw and read the title without the slightest hesitation. This test and many experiments of the kind were tried and repeated; and the demonstration of vision, independent of the physical organs of sense, was clear and unquestionable."

On subsequent occasions Andrew Jackson Davis had experiences which carried him considerably farther afield. As he watched people die and saw their spirits leave their bodies, he said, "Death is but a door which opens into new and more perfect existence. It is a Triumphal Arch through which man's immortal spirit passes at the moment of leaving the outer world to depart for a higher, a sublimer, and a more magnificent country. And there is really nothing more painful or repulsive in the natural process of dying . . . than there is in passing into a quiet, pleasant, and dreamless slumber."

"What is customarily termed death," he says, "is but a birth of the spirit from a lower into a higher stage; that an inferior body and mode of existence are exchanged for a superior body and corresponding endowments and capabilities of happiness."

If we've been wondering about other planets in connection with life after death, here is a very elaborate description given by a friend of Davis' who has passed over: "How universal is the Universe! The innumerable Empires of Worlds about me supply every pure desire with its proper and complete gratification.

"The elements, which flow between one planet or world,

and another, correspond to the bodies of water which divide, yet unite, countries and hemispheres on your earth. These planets are our various countries. On each the inhabitants are different, but only in degrees of growth. Their laws and customs differ; but the difference is always in accordance with their relative position in the infinite system of progressive development. There is no antagonism here, only a divine emulation; no absolute discord, only relative degrees of harmony.

"We travel to each other's country or planet, just as you travel to each other's village or city. Our Empire is vast— our Government is spiritual—our law is love—and our obedience brings wisdom and happiness."

Davis accepted without question all this hyperbolic heavenly happiness but he wondered why the inhabitants of the different spheres he was describing were called angels. "Because," his friend replied, "the chief employment of spirits is the transmission of thoughts, truths, and affections, from circle to circle and from sphere to sphere. Happiness and progression consist in receiving and imparting—in unfolding and assisting others to unfold—in seeking the Great Divinity, and in imparting to others the results of our celestial investigations; angels, therefore, are messengers of thoughts, truths, and affections.

"The angels' home is truly a 'house of many mansions.' The spirit-land is indeed a country of undying charms and positive attractions . . . Those spirits which emanate from the earth, or from any other planet in the universe, are introduced into that society for which they entertain the most congenial sympathies or affections . . . Undeveloped individuals who are interested more in personal gratifications than in causing happiness to others are, immediately after death, by the principle of spiritual affinity, introduced into the first sphere or circle of the second sphere; which circle is termed Self Love.

"And lonely individuals—or those who are unmarried in truth (although they may have been attached on earth by human laws to some companion), and who are yet seeking (because they feel drawn toward) their proper and eternal associates—such are introduced into the second circle in the same sphere; and this circle is called Conjugal Love.

"Some minds learn great truths in a few days; but many who pass from the earth into the spirit world . . . are very slow to disrobe their minds of errors; and such are detained in the first circle until all their theories are displaced by truths; their faith by knowledge; their pride by humility; their uncharitableness by fraternal love; and their terrestrialism by realization of spirituality and permanent realities."

Davis' communicant said to tell the earth's inhabitants to free themselves from all unkindness, jealousy, animosity, prejudice, and discord before they depart the earth, because the angels can see the motives and read the minds of all new spirits. They start right in to help those who need help to unfold the sweeter elements of their natures.

We all realize a constant failure to live up to our highest ideals, but Davis brings out a good psychological point when he says, "We cannot hold anyone responsible for not choosing a good that is beyond his vision. All men are essentially good in their inner beings." All are striving for something which seems good to them—what seems to them the best good within their power of attainment. Go among thieves and you will find among them a complete skepticism as to any motives but purely selfish and mercenary ones. They are striving for what seems to them the greatest value, money. Show them the value of justice and teach them to love it and they will limit their desire for money accordingly. Mere punishment by their fellow men is neither just nor useful for reformation. Davis's way: "We all have the same problem to solve in ourselves; first to extend our perceptions of higher values, then to live up to them by learning to love them."

The best news I've heard lately is all this talk about how busy we can keep in spirit planes. I've never been one for harp strumming all day long and loafing about on clouds.

"The universal principle of progress works constantly

and inevitably in the character of everyone," Davis says. All are destined to noble and beautiful development, sooner or later. It is not safe to despise any human being. He may overtake you in life's journey, when it will pain you to remember that you treated with contempt the undeveloped being who now walks beside you in strength and beauty."

CHAPTER THIRTEEN

More Nonbelievers

"Is it not clear and patent to you now that there is a great cloud of witnesses who dwell beyond your ken and yet in your midst as raindrops in an all-pervading ocean of spirit; not absorbed in Nirvana, as the Esoterics assert, nor lost to a sense of Personality and Individuality, but actual individual drops . . . ?"

This is another of those statements which came from the spirit world through automatic writing, and so you may take it or leave it as evidence. It is a remark made by one of the monks who allegedly helped to find the locations of the buried walls and foundations of the buildings at Gastonbury Abbey in England. F. Bligh Bond, an ecclesiastical architect, had a friend who did automatic writing. When the two of them attempted to learn about the Abbey from the spirits of monks who said they had lived there many centuries before, all the information they acquired proved to be true. The monks said they either remained at the site where they had been so peaceful on earth, or often revisited it. In *The Gate to Remembrance,* from which the above passage was taken, and several other books, Bond wrote of his communicants and the directions he received from them.

Another alleged spirit writer, who has a lot going for her in the way of proof of her reality, is Patience Worth. In 1913 Mrs. Pearl Lenore Curran of St. Louis, Missouri, discovered Patience via the ouija board. Or perhaps I should say that Patience discovered Mrs. Curran, who had spent a year receiving only the most banal ouija talk until the day when Patience wrote the statement of her existence. After this she wrote very frequently for a period of years; and eventually she began to speak through Mrs. Curran's mouth in order to give her messages more easily.

Patience said that she had been born in 1603 in Devonshire, England. She came to America after she was a grown woman, and was killed by an Indian in 1649. She always spoke entirely in an Elizabethan idiom, and had a great deal of knowledge about the period of time in which she claimed to have lived—information which Mrs. Curran did not normally know. There have been claims, of course, by those who have not truly studied the subject, that Pearl Curran had a split personality; but we won't get into an argument about that here. Suffice it to quote the statement of Dr. Walter Franklin Prince, executive research officer of the Boston Society for Psychical Research, who investigated her case thoroughly on the spot during the time when Patience was most productive. In his book *The Case of Patience Worth* Dr. Prince says:

"This is the thesis which I formulate after ten months' study of the data: EITHER OUR CONCEPT OF WHAT WE CALL THE SUBCONSCIOUS MUST BE RADICALLY ALTERED, SO AS TO INCLUDE POTENCIES OF WHICH WE HITHERTO HAVE HAD NO KNOWLEDGE, OR ELSE SOME CAUSE OPERATING THROUGH BUT NOT ORIGINATING IN THE SUBCONSCIOUSNESS OF MRS. CURRAN MUST BE ACKNOWLEDGED. In the former case we normalize what hitherto would have seemed 'supernormal' (in the same manner as hypnosis, which a hundred years ago was thought to involve a supernormal claim, has been normalized); in the second case we admit the supernormal."

Since in this book, in order to discuss the evidence for immortality intelligently, we are presuming the existence of spirits and accepting reported spirit communication without too much quibbling, let us get on with Patience's work. She was a great poet, and over the years she dictated through her medium, Mrs. Curran, millions of words—poems, short stories, and several complete novels.

About life on earth, Patience agreed with St. Paul perfectly, when she said, "There be but one quickenin'. Rebirth is of the spirit. The flesh is but a vessel in which the great God pours."

In a poem written January 3, 1920, Patience expressed thoughts with which I agree perfectly when she wrote:

"Who would become a child
If Heaven were a rebirth to infancy?
What then the game? To become
A child again with no heritage
Of memory? Then life is vain."

Another voice in the spirit-medium chorus of disbelief in reincarnation is that of Gladys Osborne Leonard, one of the world's greatest mediums. She is a serene, poised woman of common sense and integrity who has now endured the blessing, as she calls it, of mediumship for over eighty-five years. While in a trance state she has been responsible for the receiving of a fantastic amount of evidential material which has purported to come from spirit entities. On many other occasions Gladys has visited her husband, who preceded her in death. His present abode, she says, is very much like the descriptions of existence after death which have been received through other mediums.

From her personal experiences of this nature, Gladys has a firm belief that when she passes over she will immediately be met by her beloved husband and will progress with his constant companionship in future planes. The thought that she might not consciously accompany her husband and her mother and those she loves who are in the spirit world would be distressing to Mrs. Leonard. She has told me personally that she knows that she will proceed after death as herself, with all her memories, her consciousness, and her personal awareness, and that she will rejoin those she loves. It would be no pleasure to her, she says, to think that she would have to have other relationships with her husband, such as being his mother or his child in another life. She is glad that she knows from the things she has seen when she has visited him, and from what she has learned from the wise spirits she has met, that he will continue to have the same awareness of her, and to live the same role with regard to her, as he always has.

A well-known Frenchman of Allan Kardec's day, Alphonse Cahagnet published a book in 1848 in which spirits declared emphatically: "We are born and die but once; when we are in heaven it is for eternity."

In England, the famous physical medium Daniel D. Home denied and ridiculed the doctrine of reincarnation. He and Madame Blavatsky had lots of public feuding about it.

I find that today in the United States there are many mediums who do not believe in reincarnation, but they have learned not to mention it publicly; because among their sitters are so many who have taken to rebirth with enthusiasm. Perhaps after I have made this first step in the open, those who are on my side will speak up.

Some people who do not particularly like their relatives or their mates might wish to disagree with Mrs. Leonard and be reborn in order to get away from them. That plane of Conjugal Love mentioned by Andrew Jackson Davis might be the solution for them. A marriage bureau in the spirit world is a little bit too Oliver Lodgish for my taste; and yet it might be consoling at that, for those of us who have not been properly spoused on earth to believe that we may have better luck after death.

This certainly may be too earthy a belief for some, however. I think, to tell the truth, that perhaps the reason reincarnation appeals to some persons is because they want some definite scheme of survival but just can't stomach spooks.

Yet a great many people who aren't mediums and who don't have spirit communications have gone on record as believing that there is evidence for a life after death. Dr. Norman Vincent Peale, probably the best-known minister in America, is such a believer.

In 1939 news reached Peale that his mother had died unexpectedly. Shortly afterward, he sat alone in his office, numb with grief. There was a Bible on his desk. As he put his hand on it, and stared blindly out the window, he felt a pair of hands touch his head, gently, lovingly, unmistakably. The pressure lasted only an instant; then it was gone. Peale says he is convinced that his mother was permitted to reach across the gulf of death in this farewell touch.

Dr. Peale always had a questioning mind, and he tried to deal factually with this experience, reasoning that it might be a hallucination due to grief, but "I could not make myself believe this. From that moment on I have never doubted my mother's spiritual aliveness. I *know* that she lives and that she will live forever."

He says he does not have the slightest doubt concerning the truth and valadity of immortality. "I believe absolutely and certainly that when you die you will meet your loved ones and know them and be reunited with them, never to be separated again," he said, also admitting to the belief that identity of personality will continue in a greater sphere of life in which there will be no suffering or sorrow as we know them here in the physical sense. Certainly, Dr. Peale thinks there will be ongoing development, for life with no upward effort of the spirit would be incredibly dull."

Author Victor Hugo didn't pull his punches about his beliefs, either, although he kept them a secret for over thirty years. In his *Intellectual Autobiography* he says: "I am a soul. I know well that what I shall render up to the grave is not myself. That which is myself will go elsewhere. Earth, thou art not my abyss! . . . The whole creation is a perpetual ascension, from brute to man, from man to God. To divest ourselves more and more of matter, to be clothed more and more with spirit, such is the law. Each time we die we gain more of life. Souls pass from one sphere to another without loss of personality, become more and more bright . . ."

Victor Hugo also said, "When I go down to the grave I can say like many others, 'I have finished my day's work,' but I cannot say, 'I have finished my life.' My day's work will begin again the next morning. The tomb is not a blind alley; there is a thoroughfare. It closes on the twilight. It opens on the dawn."

The reason Victor Hugo did not publish his conclusions

was because he and his family were holding séances at their home on the Channel Isle of Jersey and he found it rather embarrassing. He kept orderly and detailed notes about them, which were finally published by his literary executor in 1923 in a book now out of print called *Les Tables Tournantes de Jersey* (*The Jersey Table that Turned*).

Hugo's statement above that "Each time we die we gain more of life" might seem to a reincarnationist that he believed in rebirth. But his preceding statement makes it clear that he is referring to dying as spirits do, when they pass from one sphere to another in spirit life. At this time they become less material, and farther and farther from earth with each new "incarnation." This is explained by some as the reason the "misinterpretation" of reincarnation on earth began—when spirits spoke of new incarnations in the spirit world. As Hugo put it—"The whole creation is a perpetual ascension, from brute to man, from man to God. To divest ourselves more and more of matter, to be clothed more and more with spirit, such is the law . . ." His statement here concludes, if I may be forgiven for repeating it once more with italics this time, to make my point more clear, "Souls pass *from one sphere to another without loss of personality,* become more and more bright . . ."

It does not really surprise one to find ministers and authors turning to philosophy and being convinced of immortality. But physicists—that's a different story. Yet in almost every book written by a prominent present-day physicist one finds him grappling with the problems which his science has not answered for him—the whys and wherefores of life and how to come to grips with them in the most intelligent manner.

Arthur H. Compton, who won the Nobel Prize in Physics in 1927 for his work on X-Rays and radiation, is now Distinguished Service Professor of Natural Philosophy at Washington University in St. Louis, Missouri. Throughout his writings he has maintained that religion and science are compatible and that man can and must determine his own fate. He has also stated his belief in a life after death:

It takes a whole lifetime to build the character of a noble man, he says. The adventures and disciplines of youth, the struggles, failures and successes, the pain and pleasures of maturity, the loneliness and tranquility of age—these make up the fire through which the individual must pass to be forged.

In his book *The Freedom of Man* Compton goes into this further. A man trained in science has a deep-seated reluctance, he maintains, to present evidence which might only be considered as suggestive. Yet many who profess to speak for science have drawn the definite conclusion that death is the end of all. It takes but little investigation to find that this faith in the completeness of physical death is usually based upon an uncritical acceptance of a common-sense realism.

"Just as a more careful examination shows the brick to consist of a group of molecules, atoms, and electrons—a complex system of electrical fields wholly different from the commonsense picture—so the 'obviousness' of death is found to disappear when more closely studied," Compton said, allowing that while science presents no weighty evidence for life eternal, it is only fair to point out that science has found no cogent reason for supposing that what is of importance in man can be buried in a grave. The truth is that science cannot supply a definite answer to the question.

As long ago as 1900 Frederic W. H. Myers, one of the founders of the Society for Psychical Research, whom I have quoted earlier, said that telepathy and clairvoyance indisputably imply an enlarged conception of the universe, and "so soon as man is steadily conceived as dwelling in this wider range of powers, his survival of death becomes an almost inevitable corollary."

Dr. J. B. Rhine, America's most famous psychical researcher—or parapsychologist as he prefers to be called—hints at the same thing in an article in the New York *Herald-Tribune*, February 27, 1944. "Is it not then provocative, to say the least, to discover certain capacities of mind that appear to operate beyond the boundaries of space and time within which our sensorial, bodily system has to live and move? Here, surely, if ever, 'hope sees a star' and the urge toward an inquiry into the question of survival receives valuable impetus and encouragement."

Nobel prize-winning physicist Pierre Lecomte du Noüy says in *Human Destiny* that evolution always proceeds from the most highly developed organ at any given stage. Consciousness being the newest and greatest achievement of the evolutionary process, this means that from here on life will evolve toward a higher stage from the human brain, the mind, the consciousness. In other words, at the apex of evolution man has achieved a spiritual component, or soul, and from this point on, while his body may continue adapting itself to the conditions of life, it will be along the lines of this spiritual component that his evolutionary development will proceed. Dr. du Noüy says, "The destiny of man is not limited to his existence on earth and he must never forget that fact." Life, he says, did not just happen; it was willed. It is as intentional a creation as a skyscraper. And he feels that the great discoveries of tomorrow will not be in the realm of biochemistry or nuclear physics, but in the field of "the so-called psychic, the extrasensory." And so this great physicist agrees with our parapsychologists, and with those of us who are studying ESP and its various related areas as a background with which to prove immortality scientifically.

Now away from the scientific and back to spirit communication—and a book about which there is not the slightest bit of evidence from whence it came. It could have been from the subconscious mind of its writer—which must have been unusually gigantic, in that case, because *Oahspe* is a huge volume. *Oahspe* was received by automatic writing, and it took a bit of doing, believe me. It is called "A New Bible." It was written in 1881 through the mediumship of Dr. John Ballou Newbrough, a medical doctor and dentist who was also a psychical researcher for many years. Becoming disgusted with the caliber of information received through most mediums, he began to work on his own psychic development and attempted as a sincere seeker after spiritual light to purify himself in order that he might contact the highest spirits for communication. After he had worked on his own development and purification for ten years he was told by his communicants to buy one of those newly invented machines known as the typewriter. He was to sit and do his automatic writing (which came through him without his being aware of what was being said) without reading what he had received. After one year of work he was told that the book was finished and could be published. Then he read what he had written.

It was said that the word *Oahspe* means "sky, earth, and spirit." The book is supposed to be a sacred history of the dominions of the higher and lower heavens on the earth for the past 24,000 years, together with a synopsis of cosmogony of the universe, the creation of the planets, the creation of man, the unseen worlds, the labor and glory of gods and goddesses [those whom Andrew Jackson Davis and others refer to as the highest angels] in the etherean heavens, with new commandments of Jehovih (sic) to man of the present day. The reader was warned to be critical in reading the book and never to accept anything whatever as the gospel truth. This, to me, gives more credibility to this work than anything else it could have said. Those persons and books which claim to have all the answers and to be the absolute truth always frighten me off immediately.

Even though *Oahspe*, like most other spirit scripts, could do with a lot of judicious editing, it is a book which has given great help to many people. In the Book of Jehovih (God, of course, the Highest of all), Chapter VI, line 21, this statement occurs: "And each and every man-child and woman-child born into life will I quicken with a new spirit, which shall proceed out of Me at the time of conception. Neither will I give to any spirit of the higher or lower heaven power to enter a womb or a foetus of a womb, and be born again."

In another place in *Oahspe* it is stated that a spirit takes a physical body only once *with one exception:* if a strong earthbound spirit determined to join again the earth-dwellers can find one whose soul is only weakly joined to his physical being, he can shove out the consciousness of the unfortunate individual and take him over, living his life for him. This is called possession, or obsession; and those who make a habit of doing this are called "professional reincarnators" according to *Oahspe*. A person, it says, who dies with the firm determination to enter the world of physical activity again can be a source of danger to those on earth, therefore, because of this possibility.

CHAPTER FOURTEEN

Case Histories Indicative of Reincarnation

Those who are looking for some kind of genuine evidence for the truth of reincarnation always point to certain curious phenomena: the instances where children claim to remember past lives. India, where the belief in rebirth is prevalent, has a number of such cases, some of which have been interesting psychical researchers for years. They know that something definitely supernormal is occurring in most of these cases, but they do not have enough evidence to explain it as either reincarnation, possession, or extrasensory perception.

Shanti Devi is the most famous of these Indian children, and her story has been used countless times in countless books, including several of my own, so I won't go into it in detail here. Suffice it to say that Shanti was born in 1926 in Delhi and began from the age of three to talk about her husband and son in the town of Muttra, about eighty miles away. She said her name had been Lugdi, and that she had been married to a man named Kedar Nath Chaubey. As the years went by, Shanti added to her story, stating that she had been born in 1902, that her husband was a cloth merchant, and that she had given birth to a son and then had died ten days later.

By the time she was nine years old Shanti was so insistent about her former life that her parents, who had not wished to encourage her because of the prevalent belief that reborn children always died young, finally wrote to Muttra for confirmation of her story. It was learned that what she had said was true. She was taken to Muttra, where she recognized all the people that Lugdi would have known and knew the exact location of the house where Lugdi had lived. She even told Chaubey where she had hidden some money under the floor, and he admitted that he had found it after Lugdi's death. Shanti Devi made at least twenty-four statements of memories which were verified. She is still living in India, but as she has grown older her memories of her past life have not been as strong as they once were. This too is characteristic of such children.

It is interesting to note that some young people in other countries have also claimed to have these past life memories. Katsugoro was a Japanese boy, about whom American poet Lafcadio Hearn wrote. He began when he was about eight years old to call himself Tozo, saying that had been his name in another life a few years before. He claimed to have been the son of a farmer named Kyubei and his wife Shidzu of a village called Hodokubo. He said his father had died and his mother had married a man called Hanshiro, that Tozo had died of smallpox at the age of six, a year after his father died. Katsugoro gave details of Tozo's burial and described his former parents and their house. He was eventually taken to the village of Hodokubo where, unaccompanied by anyone from the village, he led the way to Tozo's house and recognized it and his parents. He pointed to a shop and a tree nearby, saying that they had not been there before, which was true. Altogether Katsugoro made sixteen statements which were true, and responsible witnesses made numerous affidavits to this effect.

Vidyabati Devi was the Hindu wife of Mangal Deo Sharma and "the best wife a man ever had," according to her husband. "She is my salvation," he said. "She thinks only of how I may be happy, healthy, and prosperous." But when Vidyabati was a child, her memories were all of her previous mate. When she was less than three, she used to make mud patties and tell her mother to give them to Punditji. When asked who Punditji was, she said it was her husband. Now, everyone knows that children invent imaginary playmates, so her mother laughed it off at first. But parents in India pay more attention, because of this belief in rebirth; so when Vidyabati named her former

113

husband as Dr. Vasudev Sharma and described his home in another city and her life while married to him, her mother made it a point to find out what was up. She learned that there really was such a man in the city the child had described and that the details of his life were exactly as she had depicted.

Dr. Sharma was interviewed by writer Sushil Chandra Bose, who told about it in *Jatismar Kathá—a Book on Reincarnation*. Dr. Sharma was an old man, but he remembered Vidyabati well. He had been taken to meet her anonymously when she was seven years old. As soon as she saw him she put a cloth over her head as Indian women do in the presence of their husbands. Then she whispered his name. She was able to identify so many things and to tell him so much that was intimate between himself and his fourth wife who had died that Dr. Vasudev Sharma became firmly convinced that Vidyabati had been his wife in her past incarnation.

Now, unless reincarnation is true, what kind of other possible explanations are there for such unusual happenings? Well, of course, there is always fraud. Perhaps the parents of the child wish to make money off of him and so they coach him about some individual of whom they read in the newspapers. This apparently has happened on occasion, but in most historical cases there is such good evidence that fraud can be ruled out. Unconscious fraud provides a slightly less plausible hypothesis—the possibility that the child may have mentioned a past life as someone he read or heard about and then his parents unconsciously added more to the tale as they retold it. There are times as we well know when an incident gets so embroidered in the telling as to become almost fraudulent.

Psychical researchers, whatever their own beliefs about reincarnation or possession, find the stories of children who claim to remember past lives increasingly interesting and worthy of study. So many such cases can't all be fraud or wishful thinking on the part of families trying to make something out of their children's games of make-believe. There may be more realistic theories than reincarnation to account for them, and the researchers are trying to formulate some. So far they haven't been very successful. The man who has done the most investigating of claimed past life memories is Dr. Ian Stevenson of the University of Virginia School of Medicine. His book *Twenty Cases Suggestive of Reincarnation* is the best and most comprehensive work on the subject.

Personification is one of the alternative theories suggested by Dr. Stevenson. Once in a while a hypnotized subject who has been asked to reveal information about a former life will produce quantities of material which he would not seem to have had any normal way of knowing. There is considerable discussion about the source of it. But in most cases when a subject is hypnotized and regressed to a former life, he is obviously personifying, or acting out the role, to please the hypnotist. Dr. Stevenson recognizes that there have been some cases demonstrating that some individuals can "personify" buried memories during hypnosis. "But," he asks, "have buried memories ever been found to account for any cases of children who claim to have lived before? I can only say that so far, in an experience of personally investigating many cases of such children, I have not encountered such a case."

Perhaps these children have somehow tapped into Edgar Cayce's Akashic Records? If all human thoughts and actions have been recorded on a constantly moving cosmic television set, perhaps this is how the child gets his information.

Psychologists now understand something which is referred to as racial memory: the similarity of symbols in dreams and myths of all races has given them the idea that in the subconscious portion of our minds, hidden from access except under special circumstances, lie dispositions and memories carried over from the past of the human race and inherited by us in our genes.

This theory explains why the female of certain animal species knows instinctively how to care for her young, even though she may have been raised away from her own mother's influence and example. It also explains general aptitudes of human behavior, and even perhaps the passing-on within the same family of special traits or skills. Yet the extension of this idea to account for the apparent memories of former lives encounters serious obstacles, because these children are almost never descendants of the deceased individuals they claim to be. They usually belong to another family in another town. "This would make impossible any transmission of information from the first to the second person along genetic lines," Dr. Stevenson says.

It might be possible for the child to have received his information about the former life through ESP. Relatives still mourning the deceased might unconsciously be sending thoughts which are picked up telepathically by the youngster, or he might have clairvoyantly gleaned the information from the tombstone or from court records. (This certainly would not be much of an explanation for those little three-year-olds, unless children learn to read unusually early in India.)

Despite its complications, Professor C. T. K. Chari of Madras Christian College in India, another psychical researcher who has spent time studying these cases, leans toward extrasensory perception as the answer to the puzzle. That strange capacity of the mind, he believes, "may here be in operation in some form more powerful than we have yet perceived anywhere else." Yet again, Chari says, "Why is a spiritistic interpretation ruled out?" This, then, would take us right back to *Oahspe* and its idea of "professional reincarnationists."

That such a thought can be taken seriously by critical observers shows how far the world is now advancing toward spiritism (not Kardec's Spiritism, but the scientific study of spirit evidence). Lest you still think it is not a fairly widespread concept, consider a statement made by Dr. Godfrey Raupert of London. He was delegated by Pope Pius X to lecture to Catholic audiences in America on the subject. To them he said, in substance, "It is no longer possible to put the subject of psychic phenomena aside. The scientific men all over the world have recognized spirit-

116

ism as a definite and real power, and to shelve it is a dangerous policy. Consequently the Pope has asked me to tell Catholics the attitude to take toward the subject . . . The Church admits the reality of these phenomena and their external intelligences; in fact, it has always admitted their reality. The problem at present is to discover the nature of the intelligence. We are now on the borderland of new discoveries which may revolutionize the world. It is not the time yet for an explanation of all the phenomena. We must suspend our judgment until the subject is better known. The study of spiritism is a new one and therefore dangerous . . . A partial knowledge of the subject may cause grave dangers." (He was referring here, of course, to the dangers of possession or strong influence from undesirable spirits.)

How else would it be possible to explain the story of the rebirth of Alexandrina Samona except as some kind of evidence for some kind of immortality? The little girl, daughter of Dr. Carmelo Samona and his wife Adela of Palermo, Sicily, died on March 15, 1910. Three nights after her death her mother dreamed that Alexandrina had appeared to her and said, "Mother, don't cry any more. I haven't left you; I have only gone away for a while. Look, I shall become little like this." The child in the dream showed her mother the likeness of a complete little embryo. Then she added, "You're going to have to begin to suffer again on account of me." Three nights later, the same dream occurred again.

A friend suggested to Madame Samona that this meant that Alexandrina would reincarnate in a new baby. But the mother had had an operation which was supposed to make it impossible for her to have any more children.

Several days later, at a time when the Samonas were especially grieving for Alexandrina, three sharp knocks were heard which were inexplicable by normal means. It was decided to hold a family seance, and when this was done, two spirits manifested, claiming to be Alexandrina and an aunt of hers who had died years before. Alexandrina's spirit said she had shown herself to her mother in

117

her dreams and that she had also made the three raps. She said she would be reborn with a twin sister before Christmas.

On November 22, 1910, Madame Samona gave birth to twin daughters. One of them so closely resembled Alexandrina that she was named Alexandrina II. She turned out to be calm, neat, and content to play by herself, as her sister had been. She also had, like her namesake, a congested left eye, an excessive discharge from the sebaceous glands of the right ear, and noticeable facial asymmetry. Also she had little habits like Alexandrina's: she was left-handed, she hated cheese, she insisted that her hands should always be clean, and she enjoyed playing endlessly at folding, tidying, and arranging her clothes or a handkerchief or any linen she could get her hands on.

An incident that was particularly well remembered by Mrs. Samona occurred when the twins were ten years old and were told that they were going to be taken to Monreale, where they had never been before. Alexandrina said she had too been to Monreale, with her mother and a lady, who had horns. She described the large statue on the roof of the church there, and she said they had met some little red priests in the town. Then Madame Samona recalled that some months before the death of Alexandrina I, she and the little girl had gone to Monreale, accompanied by a lady who had disfiguring wens on her forehead (which the child had thought of as horns). At that time they had seen a group of young Greek priests with blue robes ornamented with red.

His whole experience with his two daughters who shared the same memories, and possibly the same body, was so unusual to Dr. Samona that he wrote down his own recollections, and also acquired the attestations of several other persons who were personally acquainted with the facts—in particular his wife, his own sister, his wife's uncle, and a preacher to whom his wife had related the prediction of the rebirth before it was fulfilled.

As Dr. Stevenson points out, "So far as we concern ourselves with evidence for survival, we are not obliged to suppose that *every* case suggestive of rebirth needs to be explained as an instance of reincarnation." However, certain cases, like Alexandrina's have specific idiosyncrasies or congenital birthmarks or deformities which were almost identical with those of the persons whom the children professed to be. In Alexandrina's case, she herself is alleged to have caused these things to happen to the new child in order to prove that it was herself reborn. Dr. Stevenson believes that such cases as he has personally investigated of this nature give better evidence favorable to reincarnation than any others. With strict scientific objectivity, he does not claim that they *prove* reincarnation. He does, however, find them quite impressive.

CHAPTER FIFTEEN

Possession of Mortals by Spirit Entities

In *Heaven and Hell* Emanuel Swedenborg discusses the prevalence of spirit influence—it being much greater than even believers in it normally realize. He said that the habit of spirits speaking to humans was not encouraged "up there" for several reasons, one of which is that those spirits who are not highly developed would not know how to do it right. He says, "If a spirit should speak with a man from his own memory, then the man would not know otherwise than that the things which he then thought were his own, when yet they were the spirit's; it is like the recollection of a thing, which yet the man never heard or saw. That it is so has been given to me to know from experience. From this some of the ancients had the opinion that after some thousands of years they should return into their former life, and into all its acts, and also that they had returned. They concluded it from this, that sometimes there occurred to them a recollection, as it were, of things which they never saw or heard; and this came to pass because spirits flowed from their own memory into their ideas or thought."

Other spirit communicators have stated that as much as one-third of what we believe we are thinking comes to us *externally* instead of from our own minds. It is frequently earthbound spirits who pay attention to us; but also those who love us who have died may be attempting to help us. If we would be more receptive to constructive thoughts, we are told, we could receive a great deal of help from them. If the thoughts are negative and not helpful, instead of encouraging them, we should dismiss them and close our minds to further thinking of like vein. This will keep away the unwanted entities who might try to intrude themselves upon us. Knowledge of this possibility is protection against it, we are informed by the progressed informants who communicate.

For the lowest type of earthbound entities Swedenborg uses the words "natural" or "corporal" spirits. He writes, "When these come to a man they do not conjoin themselves with his thought, like other spirits, but enter into his body, and occupy all his senses, and speak through his mouth, and act through his members, believing at the time that all things of the man are theirs. These are the spirits that obsess man."

Ian Stevenson points out that we have evidence that such a thing as possession can happen—and he is not now referring to memories of past lives or of earthbound spirits taking over but to historical material in the files of parapsychology. "By this I mean," he says, "that in certain mediumistic experiences the body of the medium becomes so completely controlled by another personality that observers believe it occupied by a deceased personality whose special characteristics they claim to identify."

An example of communication of this sort is given in my book *The Mediumship of Mrs. Leonard* in which, in order to show his personality as naturally as in life, one entity who communicated through the body of the entranced Gladys Osborne Leonard displayed a severe attack of asthma. The elderly Scotch gentleman maintained an unusually strong control of the medium for forty minutes. During this time he spoke in robust and fully audible tones of a surprisingly masculine quality, interrupted at intervals by paroxysms of coughing and wheezing characteristic of the bronchial asthma which had afflicted him during his lifetime. The entire effect was unquestionably that of a man in bad shape. Except for the wheezing, the voice did not seem strained or forced, and Mrs. Leonard awoke with no signs of exhaustion. She entered immediately into conversation without a trace of hoarseness, and she was as devoid of all cough or chest obstruction as she had been before the sitting. The sitters recognized the man by the personal things he said, by his inflections, and also by this reproduction of his famous asthma. To say the least, they were slightly overcome!

Sometimes a strongly psychic individual, who may be a potential medium without knowing, may give indications of such possession. An illiterate maid in the home of the sister of Senator Quintin Paredes of the Philippines was reported in the Philippine *Free Press* to have experienced such possession intermittently for a long time. Whenever she went into a trance she was taken over by some entities who did not tell who they were but who had an unusual amount of knowledge. Sometimes when her own personality was "out cold" she could speak perfect English, French, or German, although normally she knew none of these languages. During registration days for voters, she would become entranced. Even though she didn't know how to read or write, she would be able to go to the polls in her trance state, qualify on the examinations, and vote, filling out the ballots without help. When she was told afterwards what had happened, she would quite naturally be baffled, for she had no recollection of anything she did while possessed.

Once, when Senator Paredes was visiting his sister, accompanied by other members of the legislative body of the Philippines, the entranced maid spoke in the voice of Paredes' own son, Lieutenant Isidro Paredes, who had enlisted in the R.A.F., and had been killed in action in England. Through the maid he gave details of his death and burial and described his property left in London. This was verified four years later when his father visited that city.

When possession occurs with a medium, or a mediumistically inclined individual, it is usually sporadic; he goes into trance and some entity takes him over for a brief period, then he returns to normal. Possession also occurs, we are told, among those who are weak-willed and lacking in strength of character or are frequently in a state of little control, such as a drunken stupor. The possession is then only temporary and goes away when the individual comes back to normal. Possession or obsession may be continuous, however, coming and going over a long period of time, as illustrated in the Gifford-Thompson case. An engraver named Thompson suddenly found himself impressed by a powerful compulsion to paint certain scenes which rose vividly into his mind. He had never been an artist, but when he attempted to put these down, they were very professional and very good. Also, they looked exactly like the pictures of Robert Swain Gifford, who had died about six months before. Thompson had known Gifford slightly, but he had no reason to believe that he should be so favored with his attentions.

Thompson said, "I remember having the impression that I was Mr. Gifford himself, and I would tell my wife before starting out that Mr. Gifford wanted to go sketching, although I did not know at that time that he had died early in the year." From time to time afterward Thompson heard a voice urging him to get on with the sketching and painting. The influence began to cause serious interference with the engraver's regular occupation, for he would take journeys to other parts of the country under the influence of the impulse to paint certain scenes which were favorites of the deceased artist's. During most of this time, Thompson continued to be aware of his own identity; yet on one occasion at least he had a period of complete amnesia when he did not remember a thing that he had done while under the influence of the Gifford personality.

Such a case as this would seem to parallel the experiences of those children who claim to remember past lives. I am not sure that any of them are taken over permanently by these obsessing personalities, but they certainly may be influenced so strongly (as Mr. Thompson was) as to think they are the deceased personality at least part of the time. Since they are so small, they cannot understand what is happening to them or explain how it feels. (For that matter, most adults who experience this do not-seem to be able to understand it very well, either.)

There are several instances among these children, however, which are indicative of complete possession, one of them in our own country. The case of Lurancy Vennum definitely does not indicate reincarnation, because the child was thirteen when her experience—which was only temporary—occurred; but it was complete and entire while it went on. This is such an excellent example of possession, and was so carefully written up at the time it happened, that it is necessary to go into it here again, although it is definitely a rerun.

In Watseka, Illinois, in 1878, Mary Lurancy Vennum began to have what were called fits. It appeared that she went into trance and a procession of spirit oddballs took her over. One minute she might say she was Willie Canning, and she would talk and act like a fresh young man. A short time later she would claim to be an old woman named Katrina Hogan. Then she would sit with mussed hair and slatternly posture, actually looking like an old hag.

Dr. E. W. Stevens, a medical man who was also a spiritualist, was brought in to investigate her condition. After calming her, he suggested she should try to find some strong spirit who could control her and keep the intruders away. The child mentioned the names of several deceased persons whom she said she could see. Then she indicated that there was one, a Mary Roff, who particularly wanted to help her.

Mary Roff was a local girl who had died at the age of eighteen, when Lurancy was about fifteen months old. It was decided that Mary should control the body of Lurancy until her reserves were strong enough that she could protect herself from the invasion of earthbound entities. The transfer of ownership of the body of Lurancy Vennum was accomplished the next day. Lurancy's own consciousness disappeared and in its stead came the personality, mind, and memories of Mary Roff. For the next three months this child who looked like Lurancy Vennum spoke and acted and thought and remembered like this other girl who had died thirteen years before.

Obviously uncomfortable in the Vennum home after the change had been made, the girl was allowed to go and live with Mary's parents. There she knew everything and everyone Mary had known in the past. She recognized and called by name those who were friends of her family. She remembered scores, even hundreds of incidents that had transpired during Mary's life.

One evening while the child was out in the yard, Mr. Roff suggested that his wife find a certain velvet headdress that Mary had worn the last year before she died. He told her to lay it out and say nothing about it, to see if it would be recognized. Lurancy (as Mary) soon came in, and immediately exclaimed as she approached the stand, "Oh, there is my headdress I wore when my hair was short!" She then asked, "Ma, where is my box of letters? Have you got them yet?" Mrs. Roff dug out a box long stored in the attic. Examining it, the girl said, "Oh, Ma, here is a collar I tatted. Why didn't you show me my letters and things before?"

An on-the-spot report of the incidents of this case was eventually compiled by Dr. Richard Hodgson of the Society for Psychical Research. He went to Watseka about twelve years after the big event and interviewed members of both families and their friends. Objective as he was, after his investigation Hodgson felt impelled to suggest that there seemed a strong likelihood that the highly controversial occurrence he was recording had actually transpired as told to him.

When Hodgson visited Mrs. Minerva Alter, Mary Roff's sister, she assured him that the mannerisms and behavior of Lurancy Vennum when under the ostensible control of Mary Roff strikingly resembled those of her sister. The real Lurancy had known Mrs. Alter previously, having met her casually at school, but she knew her as "Mrs. Alter." While under the control of Mary she embraced Mrs. Alter affectionately and called her "Nervie," Mary's pet name for her for many years.

Lurancy-Mary stayed at Mrs. Alter's home for a while, and almost every hour of the day some trifling incident of Mary's life was recalled by her. One morning she said, "Right over there by the currant bushes is where Allie greased the chicken's eye." This incident had happened several years before Mary's death. Mrs. Alter remembered very well their cousin Allie treating the sick chicken's eye with oil. Allie now lived in Peoria, Illinois, and Lurancy had never known her.

One morning Mrs. Alter asked the girl if she remembered a certain old dog they had owned. Lurancy replied, "Yes, he died over there," pointing out the exact spot where the pet had breathed his last. The Roff family considered accumulations of little things like this to be incontrovertible evidence that Mary was actually visiting them in this other body, no matter that such a thing had never occurred before in history—to the knowledge of anyone present.

When the term of Mary's tenure was up, it was declared (by spirit presence, evidently) that Lurancy was entirely healed and could return to her body. This she did, and she was well from then on. The Roffs and Vennums had become friends—this experience of sharing a daughter had, not surprisingly, brought them close together. For some years afterwards, until Lurancy was married and had left home, whenever the parents visited together Lurancy would abdicate temporarily in favor of Mary so that she could have a chat with her mother and father.

A priceless story like this doesn't come along very often, and we are fortunate in having not only the report of Dr. Hodgson's interview, but a thorough account of the entire episode written by Dr. Stevens right at the time it happened. "The Watseka Wonder" is undoubtedly the best possession case on record.

But, now, do we have anything even remotely to compare with this among our stories of children with memories of "past lives"? Yes, we have the case of Jasbir, which is

126

exactly like Shanti Devis and the others with *one* difference, and that difference puts it in Lurancy Vennum's class—because Jasbir was *three years old* when he became "inhabited" by another entity.

Jasbir, son of Sri Girdhari Lal Jat of Rasulpur, India, died of smallpox in the spring of 1954, when he was three-and-a-half years of age. Instead of burying him immediately, as was the custom, his father and friends waited until morning, and by then the child was stirring again, feebly. So they didn't bury him at all.

He slowly came back to consciousness; but he was not able to speak for some days, and it was weeks before he could express himself clearly. Then he spoke in a different dialect altogether. He stated firmly that he was Sobha Ram, son of Sri Shankar Lal Tyagi of Vehedi, and that he was a Brahmin. He would no longer eat the low caste food served by his parents, who were Jats. He showed a remarkable transformation in behavior, acting haughty and unpleasant; and he would have starved himself had not a kind Brahmin neighbor undertaken to feed him. This she did for about a year and a half, and then gradually Jasbir began to eat with his family.

Among his memories of life in Vehedi, Jasbir told about how he had died. He said that he had eaten some poisoned sweets at a wedding procession and had become giddy and had fallen off the chariot on which he was riding. He had suffered a head injury in the fall, and death had followed some hours later. When the little boy Jasbir was finally taken to Vehedi, he recognized all the people Sobha Ram would have known, and he gave a vast amount of other information which was correct. The child was much happier in Vehedi and so from time to time his family would let him go there to visit. Dr. Ian Stevenson called on him twice in 1961 and 1964, and interviewed most of the witnesses in the case. He believes the information he received to be genuine.

The difference between reincarnation and possession, Dr. Stevenson says, lies in the extent of displacement of the primary personality achieved by the influence of the "entering" personality. The distinction he makes is this: "In short, if the previous personality seems to associate itself with the physical organism at the time of conception or during embryonic development, we speak of reincarnation; if the association between previous personality and physical organism only comes later, we speak of possession."

Of course, he is not here considering the prime difference between reincarnation and possession, which is that in reincarnation it is the same soul which is purported to be reborn into another body. In possession it is just the opposite—a deceased soul or spirit occupies the body of someone living on earth. Spirit communicants make no distinction as to when the spirit enters the body, and so according to them it could enter the foetus as easily as it could enter the newborn child. Therefore, the cases which Dr. Stevenson believes put a limitation on the theory of possession— those involving unusual birthmarks and knowledge of skills which the deceased entity had—do *not* offer stumbling blocks, according to alleged spirit sources.

A very good example of this is the case of Corliss Chotkin, Jr., which was investigated by Dr. Stevenson personally. The story begins with Victor Vincent, a full-blooded Tlingit Indian who died in Angoon, Alaska, in the spring of 1946. His niece, Mrs. Corliss Chotkin, Sr., of Sitka, and her husband had always made Vincent welcome and he had spent much time with them before his death. Once he said to his niece, "I'm coming back as your next son . . . You'll know it's me when you see these scars." He pulled up his shirt and showed her a scar on his back from an operation. It even had the small round holes alongside made by the stitches. Then he pointed to a small scar on the right side at the base of his nose.

These Indians have a belief in reincarnation, and Victor Vincent had decided to pick out a good new home even before he left his present life. In 1947, about eighteen months after his death, Mrs. Chotkin gave birth to a boy, who was named Corliss Chotkin, Jr. At his birth he had two marks on his body which were exactly the same shape and location as the scars on Victor Vincent's body. One day when Corliss, Jr., was just learning to talk he said to his mother, "Don't you know me? I'm Kahkody." This was the tribal name of Victor Vincent. When Corliss, Jr., was two years old and being wheeled along the street in Sitka by his mother, he recognized a stepdaughter of Victor Vincent, and called out her name, "Susie." He showed great excitement and jumped up and down, crying. "There's my Susie." The little boy also recognized William, the son of Victor Vincent. Mrs. Chotkin did not know William was in town, but on the street Corliss, Jr., spotted him and said, "There's William, my son."

When Corliss, Jr., was three he noticed Victor Vincent's widow on the street. He said, "That's the old lady," just as Vincent would have done. The boy also called her name, Rose. He recognized others as well, and when he grew older he told about two episodes in the life of Victor Vincent which he would have had no normal way of knowing. Many of his likes and dislikes and habits were similar to Vincent's.

About the age of nine, Ian Stevenson writes, Corliss made fewer statements about a previous life. At the time of Stevenson's interviews in 1962, Corliss was fifteen years old. He then claimed he remembered nothing of the previous life. Dr. Stevenson obtained the testimony of several people about the curious evidence that the boy was so much like Victor Vincent, but he still tried to consider every possible explanation other than a supernormal one. However, he says that if other explanations do not account for the facts, "then we must suppose that he somehow had access to the mind of Victor Vincent, that mind being either still discarnate, and 'possessing' him, or reincarnated and continuous with his own personality."

But in thinking about the evidence for such curious instances as this, Dr. Stevenson seems to conclude that the birthmark on the young boy supposes an influence prior to birth, "but possession supposes such an influence after birth with attempts to displace partially or completely the personality which participated in the shaping of the physical organism antenatally." This is an assumption on Dr. Stevenson's part of facts which certain communicating entities declare to be untrue. They maintain that it is equally as possible for a determined spirit entity to enter the baby's foetus when it begins to form as it is to enter the body at birth. Thus the spirit's would be the personality which participated in the shaping of the physical organism before birth.

That a spirit can so enter the mother before birth of her child is suggested by a story concerning a certain Melanesian spirit called a Nopitu. In the evening when a party of natives was sitting around the fire, the Nopitu would begin to talk and sing in a voice so small and clear and sweet that once heard it never could be forgotten. Then it would say, "I am going." They would call it, and it was gone. Then a woman would feel it come to her and sit upon her knee. She would hear it cry, "Mother! mother!" She would know it, and carry it in a mat upon her back like an infant. Sometimes a woman would hear a Nopitu say, "Mother, I am coming to you," and she would feel the spirit entering into her, and it would be born afterwards as an ordinary child. Such a one, named Rongoloa, was not long ago still living at Motlav, according to R. H. Codrington in *The Melanesians*.

I must confess that Dr. Stevenson is an M.D. and I am not. And he has had an opportunity to investigate personally eighteen cases in which birthmarks occurred which were reminiscent of those of a deceased person, while I have only the statements allegedly communicated from the spirit world to use for argument. Since I am quite as critical about anything which purports to come through automatism as I am about any other material claiming to be authentic, I'll promise to keep an open mind about these incidents until some proof can be acquired. Stevenson is never dogmatic either, and he cannot form a final opinion with the information now at his disposal. But, he says, "such cases of this kind as we have point toward an ideal case we may someday discover which could permit a firm choice between reincarnation and possession for that case at least."

CHAPTER SIXTEEN

Historical Cases of Possession

The belief in possession is as old as man, and is still held today by much of the human race. Obsessing or possessing spirits are frequently mentioned in the Bible—both Old and New Testaments. In First Samuel 16:23, the Good Book reads: "David took an harp, and played with his hand: so Saul was refreshed, and was well, and the evil spirit departed from him." Matthew 10:1: "Jesus gave his twelve disciples power against unclean spirits, to cast them out." Mark 1:39: "Jesus preached . . . and cast out devils." Luke 8:27, 29, 36: "A certain man which had devils a long time . . . Jesus had commanded the unclean spirit to come out of the man . . . He that was possessed of the devils was healed." Acts 19:12: "The evil spirits went out of them."

In Mark 9: 17, 21, 15–17 the story is told of the man who brought his son to Jesus, saying, "Master, I have brought unto thee my son, which hath a dumb spirit . . . And he asked his father: How long is it ago since this came unto him? And he said, Of a child . . . Jesus rebuked the foul spirit, saying unto him, Thou deaf and dumb spirit, I charge thee, come out of him, and enter no more into him. And the spirit cried, and rent him sore, and came out of him and he was as one dead; insomuch that many said, He is dead. But Jesus took him by the hand, and lifted him up; and he arose."

An interesting commentary upon this is made by T. K. Oesterreich, who has made a thorough compilation of case histories in his book *Possession*, but who has no belief in the power of spirits of the dead to enter humans. Oesterreich says that comparing these brief New Testament stories with stories of possession in later times, we find the similarity of the facts extremely surprising, while our respect for the historic truth of the Gospels is enhanced to an extraordinary degree. Excluding the story of the herd of swine Oesterreich says, Biblical narratives are of an entirely realistic and objective character, particularly in the accounts of Jesus' relation to these events. His success and failure together with those of his disciples, as well as the particulars of his cures, coincide so exactly with what we know of these states from the point of view of present-day psychology, that it seems impossible to believe we are dealing with a tradition which is factual.

Even though he is willing to admit that possession has gone on all through the history of the world, and is still predominant in primitive cultures, and that mediumship gives evidence of something supernormal, Oesterreich says that the popular conception of the present is that no psychic life takes over except in the presence of a material vehicle. Also, no spirits, either pure or only etheric in body, exist in this world. This idea, which has become one of the most firmly established constituents of our present-day outlook on life, is completely new as measured by the standard of history. It is another product of the Age of Enlightenment.

We live in an age remarkable for its mechanical and scientific improvements; but nobody can say that we were advanced philosophically by accepting materialism. And now that materialism is apparently on its way out, we must find answers to life's questions which will not be inadequate and wrong, but which will be meaningful and right for a change. Perhaps more attention to historical evidence of spirit activity and less to the conjectures of modern behaviorists might lead us to fulfillment. I am not reactionary, I am merely one who believes in facing truths wherever they present themselves, even if they should come in forms now considered to be Old Wives Tales. Let us at least look at some of the old material and see how it compares with what we are discovering in the present.

Among the writers of early Christianity are a couple who

should be quoted. St. Anthony says: "We walk in the midst of demons, who give us evil thoughts; and also in the midst of good angels. When these latter are especially present, there is no disturbance, no contention, no clamor; but something so calm and gentle it fills the soul with gladness." This could be a quotation from Swedenborg, it is so similar to his style and approach. Those who maintain these beliefs insist that humanity is surrounded by the thought influence of millions of discarnate beings, many of whom have not yet arrived at a full realization of their situation and their need to progress out of the dismal depths where they find themselves. According to Dr. Carl Wickland in *Thirty Years among the Dead*, "A recognition of this fact accounts for a great portion of unbidden thoughts, emotions, strange forebodings, gloomy moods, irritabilities, unreasonable impulses, irrational outbursts of temper, uncontrollable infatuations, and countless other mental vagaries."

This is because, according to Wickland, death does not make a saint of a sinner, nor a sage of a fool. The mentality after death is the same as before, and individuals carry with them into the spirit world their old desires, habits, dogmas, faulty teachings, indifference or disbelief in a future life, and the influence of these discarnated entities is the cause of many of the inexplicable and obscure events of earth life and of a large part of the world's misery. "Purity of life and motive, or high intellectuality, do not necessarily offer protection from obsession; recognition and knowledge of these problems are the only safeguards."

A historical case which illustrates this sort of thing is quoted from the third century A.D. Greek sophist Flavius Philostratus, in his biography of Apollonius of Tyana. He tells of a poor woman who implored the aid of the Wise Men to help her sixteen-year-old son who had been possessed for two years by an evil and lying demon.

"On what grounds do you believe this?" asked one of the Sages.

"He is," she said, "of particularly pleasing appearance; therefore, the demon loves him." He kept the boy from studying and going to school, from learning to shoot with the bow; he dragged him away to desolate places. "The boy no longer even has his own voice," she said. "He utters deep and grave sounds like a grown man. The eyes with which he looks forth are not his eyes. All this afflicts me deeply, I rend my bosom and seek to bring back my child, but he does not recognize me."

The mother goes on, "As I was preparing to come here (and I have thought of it already for a year past), the demon revealed himself to me by the mouth of my child. He declared to me that he is the spirit of a man killed in war who died loving his wife. But his wife having defiled his couch three days after his death by a new marriage, he came to loathe the love of women and has diverted all his passion on to this child. He promised me, if I consented not to denounce him before you, to do much good to my son. These promises tempted me for a little while, but now for a long time he has been the sole master in my house, where he thinks of nothing but mischief and deceit."

The Sage asked her if the child was there. "No," replied the mother. "I did all that I could to bring him; but the demon threatens to throw him into gulfs, over precipices, in a word to slay him if I accuse him before you." "Be at peace," said the Sage. "He will not slay your child when he has read this." And he drew from his bosom a letter which he gave to this woman. The letter was addressed to the demon and contained the most terrible threats toward him.

That's the end of the account. Sort of leaves you hanging, doesn't it? I wish these old stories were more complete. I'm dying to know if the letter did any good.

Well, that's possession in the old days. Here's the way it sometimes goes among primitive races, who have always believed in it—even when they sometimes also believe in reincarnation. The souls of deceased nobles become gods of the second rank in the Tonga Islands. Therefore, when a man was possessed by the spirit of Toogoo Ahoo, the late King of Tonga, he was much impressed with himself. He found it difficult to explain how he felt about it, however. When asked by anthropologists to give some details about his emotions he said "he felt himself all over in a glow of heat and quite restless and uncomfortable, and did not feel his own personal identity, but felt as if he had a mind different from his own natural mind, his thoughts wandering upon strange and unusual subjects, although perfectly sensible of surrounding objects." He was asked how he knew it was the spirit of Toogoo Ahoo. His answer was, "There's a fool! How can I tell you *how* I knew it? I felt and knew it was so by a kind of consciousness; my mind told me that it was Toogoo Ahoo."

Today if an individual says, "I hear voices telling me to kill myself," and if he seems to be out of touch with reality in other ways, we incarcerate him. "God told me to do it," is what an unfortunate woman in Maine claimed when arrested for drowning her three children. No one inquired what gave her the impression it was God, or who else it might have been who was invisibly prompting her to such a crime. She was merely put into an asylum and left there until the doctors thought she had lost her hostilities and was well enough to leave. She returned to her husband and bore him three more children. On July 2, 1967, she drowned these three children as well. The poor soul is back in an institution. No one has done anything to help her get rid of her obsession, and probably no one ever will. But psychologists say that in modern America we do not have cases of possession any more. That is for the Middle Ages and backward countries. Emotionally disturbed people in institutions are responding beautifully to tranquilizing drugs, so what matters whether we know the real causes of their initial conflicts? They were obviously purely psychological, and certainly had nothing to do with spirits of the dead and other such malarkey.

In other periods of history, and in less enlightened countries, such cases are called possession, and the entity is exorcized and the patient is quickly cured. In certain areas where there are large groups of old-fashioned Jews, the "dibbuk" is relatively common, even today. It is usually considered to be the spirit of a deceased lover who enters a girl and possesses her until removed by the rabbi of the community. Sometimes a dibbuk is some other entity, lost and homeless, who fastens upon a girl when she is in some state of weak resistance.

A story of a dibbuk in a Polish ghetto of the nineteenth century is related by Jacob Fromer in *Ghetto-Dammerung*. A man of great learning named Chaim ben Sarah read heretical works, liked to speak German and dress in European style. After he had committed acts which his family and friends considered much too far out for their times, they ostracized him. He then took to drink, frequented dubious society, and was finally imprisoned. When released his coreligionists insulted, despised, and stoned him. In the end he was unable to endure this life of shame and drowned himself.

Soon a local girl named Esther began to show the disordered hair and agitated face which were signs of possession. She spoke High-German and Latin, which she did not ordinarily know, in a harsh, rough man's voice, whose inflections were recognized as those of Chaim ben Sarah. An exorcism service was held and the rabbi extracted from the dibbuk his name, Chaim, and then asked him what had occurred after his death. He told a long story. After death he had been cast out of hell with insults and opprobrium. He wandered for a long time, but could no longer remain without habitation and finally entered into a pig.

That was not too bad. When the pig was slaughtered he passed into a horse, where he had a very poor time. It was a draught-horse, which had to work hard, receive many blows, and never eat his fill. At length he decided to try man. The occasion was propitious. He knew that Esther had illicit relations with a young man, and watched the moment when she abandoned herself to his embraces; at that instant he was permitted to enter into her. He ended his narrative by begging not to be driven out; in life and after death he had suffered so greatly that they should have pity on him and grant him a little rest.

His appeals made no impression on the rabbi, who had a job to do, and he did it. But it wasn't easy. The poor girl bore the brunt of it, having to be struck in the face in order to chastize her intruder. Then a terrible thing happened, the girl freed her hands with lightning speed and before anyone could prevent her she dealt the rabbi two resounding boxes on the ears.

Strong arms seized the girl and the rabbi struck her so furiously across her face that it streamed with blood and she collapsed with a cry and became unconscious. At this moment a noise was heard at the window as if it had been hit by a small stone. Everyone rushed toward it and discovered in one pane a hole of the size of a pea through which the spirit had fled. The girl was carried out.

Fromer had come there as an unbeliever, to study superstition, and religious dementia. The experiences of an hour left him severely shaken. In vain he told himself that the girl Esther was deluded, that she had been in touch with the dead man in his lifetime and might have imitated his voice and manner of speech. Vainly, he tried to convince himself that the rabbi had executed an illusion with involuntary comic effect. But before Fromer were thousands of men, older, more experienced and wiser. They all believed in the existence of the dibbuk, they had seen the spirit come out, they had heard the impact on the window and seen the hole in the pane. They all attested that the rabbi had times without number cured incurable sicknesses, recalled the dead to life, and brought to light inscrutable mysteries.

Oesterreich, who quotes this story, has a typical modern comment, and perhaps he is right, who knows? He says, "This narrative, which offers in other respects no peculiar psychological features, leaves the noise and the hole in the window unexplained. It is naturally insufficient to make us admit a parapsychophysical phenomenon, for it is not established that no hole existed previously and a prearranged revolver shot is not, moreover, beyond the bounds of possibility."

A young man named Frank James was written up in a New York newspaper because of the peculiar situation in which he found himself. After a fall from a motorcycle when he was ten years old, James had changed from a cheerful, affectionate, and obedient child into a surly, insolent boy, developing into a confirmed robber and criminal. After several terms in the reformatory and five years in Sing Sing prison, he was declared hopelessly psychotic and sent to the State Insane Asylum. Frank James escaped from there, and when pursued was hit on the head with a club. Falling unconscious, he was taken to a hospital. The next morning he awoke, extraordinarily changed. He was gentle and polite, showing no further indications of an unbalanced mind, and from then on he exhibited not the slightest impulse to commit crime of any kind. The newspaper article stated, according to Dr. Carl Wickland, who quotes it without attribution to name or date of the paper: "Just what happened to the mechanism of the boy's brain is not entirely understood by medical men."

This is a brief illustration of a type of case familiar to psychologists, who label them "split personalities" or variations thereof. But Dr. Wickland, who was the head of a mental institution, was vehement against what he considered to be misappellations, and bad diagnosis. This physician had discovered that his wife was a medium, and since then he had helped vast numbers of his patients by removing, with her help, the entities possessing them. His book *Thirty Years among the Dead* gives case histories of many patients who were cured. Intruding spirits were allegedly driven out of them by static electricity shock treatment. Then they entered Mrs. Wickland's body and spoke through her. They were usually spirits who had not known they had died and were very confused. Dr. Wickland told them the truth about their state and asked them to leave the patient, and they eventually always concurred. He writes that enlightened spirit entities who spoke through his wife maintained that many ignorant spirits "were attracted to the magnetic aura of mortals—although the spirit, as well as the mortal, might be unconscious of the intrusion—and thus, by obsessing or possessing their victims, they ignorantly or maliciously became the cause of untold mischief, often producing invalidism, immorality, crime, and seeming insanity."

139

An example of his case histories involves a spirit named Frank who had been intruding himself upon a patient named Mrs. Burton.

Doctor: Where did you come from?
Spirit: I don't know.
Doctor: Do you know anyone here?
Spirit: I don't see anybody I know.
Doctor: Don't you know where you came from?
Spirit: I don't know myself. How can I answer questions when I don't know?
Doctor: How long have you been dead?
Spirit: Dead! The idea! Say, what's the matter with me? I think it looks funny to see you all sitting around here. Are you having a meeting, or what is it called anyhow?
Doctor: Yes, it's a meeting. Try to tell us who you are.
Spirit: I don't know why I should tell you that.
Doctor: You are a stranger to us.
Spirit: I don't know whether I shall stay here or not. I am always peculiar among strangers, you know.
Doctor: Tell us where you came from.
Spirit: For my dear life, I don't know myself, so how can I tell you? Say, why do you hold my arm? I'm a strong man and can sit still by myself.
Doctor: I thought you were a woman.
Spirit: God above! Why do you think I'm a woman? You'll have to look again, because I am a man, sure enough, and I've always been a man. But things are funny, and I don't know; it has been so peculiar with me for some time. You know, I was walking along and then I heard some singing so I thought I'd peek in, and before I knew it I was feeling fine. You know I have not been feeling well for some time; everything has seemed unusual. I don't know what is the matter with me anyhow. Somebody said to me that if I came in where the singing was, I would find

out what is the matter with me. I've asked everybody I saw, but everybody passed by; they were
so stuck up they wouldn't talk to a fellow any
more. The people all looked like wax to me.
Dear life! I've been talking and talking and
walking and walking, and, for dear life, I could
never get anyone to answer me, or take any
notice of me before. [As a spirit he was invisible
to mortals and therefore unnoticed by them.]
You are the first one to answer any question. I
have some little peculiar kind of thing in my
throat once in a while and I can't talk, and then
I seem to get well again. But I feel queer, so
queer.

Doctor: Can you remember anything happening to you
at some time?

Spirit: Something happens every day. One time I remember one thing and another time something
else, but I don't remember anything clearly. I
cannot, for dear life, know where I am at. It is
the most peculiar thing I ever saw.

Doctor: How old are you?

Spirit: I cannot tell you that. I haven't known my age
for some time. Nobody ever asks me about that
and the natural circumstance is that I forgot.
(He hears a passing train whistle.) Why, there's
a train coming! It's a long time since I heard
that. It seems I live again for a short time. I
don't know what it is.

Doctor: Where did you live formerly? Where do you
think you are now?

Spirit: I don't know where I lived before, but right now
I am in this room with a lot of people.

Doctor: Do you know you are in Los Angeles, California?

Spirit: For dear life, no!

Doctor: Where do you think you ought to be?

Spirit: I can't seem to recall things. There are times
that I can tell you that I am a woman, and then

141

I get some kind of funny thing I don't like. (Static treatment of patient.)

Doctor: What do you get?

Spirit: When I am a woman, I have long hair, and when the hair is hanging down this funny thing begins. (Mrs. Burton was in the habit of taking her hair down during a treatment.)

Doctor: What do you mean?

Spirit: It seems like a million needles strike me, and, for God's sake, it is the worst thing I ever had in my whole life! I don't want to be a woman. I only get that funny thing when I am a woman. (Seeing Mrs. Burton in circle.) She's the one with the long hair! (To Mrs. Burton) I'm going to get you!

Doctor: Do you know that lady?

Spirit: Yes, she gets so mad at me at times and wants to chase me away.

Doctor: She probably doesn't want you around. Possibly you bother her.

Spirit: She bothers me too.

Doctor: Try to understand your condition. Cannot you realize that you are so-called dead? . . .

The spirit entity finally recalled a time in Texas when somebody struck him on the head and he had great pain. He fell down, but he got up again, having no idea that he had been killed. He didn't feel any different, but now nobody would talk to him. He thought it was about the year 1888, but instead it was 1920. He may have been wandering in darkness most of that time, until he got entangled in the aura of Mrs. Burton and could not get away from her. Finally Wickland reports, he saw his mother, among those spirits who had come to try to help him.

Spirit: Oh, look there! See! My Mother! Oh, Mother! Can you forgive me? I wasn't as you wanted me to be. Mother, will you take me? I am so tired; I

142

need your care and help. Will you take me? Oh, my Mother.

Doctor: What does she say?

Spirit: She calls me. She says, "Yes, Frank, you will come with me. I have been looking for you a long time."

His mother said she would help Frank to learn what a beautiful world there is on the other side when we have understanding. She ended, "Come, Frank, and we will go to a beautiful home in the spirit world." And Mrs. Burton, too, went home cured.

My, it's nice when a story has a happy ending!

Dr. Carl Wickland is one of the strongest arguers against reincarnation; for he insists that the spirits say it is a dangerous concept. He says, "The belief in reincarnation on earth is a fallacious one and prevents progression to higher spiritual realms after transition has been frequently declared by advanced spirits, while numerous cases of obsession which have come under our care have been due to spirits who, in endeavoring to 'reincarnate' in children, have found themselves imprisoned in the magnetic aura, causing great suffering to both their victims and themselves."

He tells about a little boy named Jack T. in Chicago who had been normal and with a good disposition until the age of five, when he began to manifest precocious tendencies and act strangely. He began to fret about things ordinarily foreign to a child's mind and acted in many ways like an adult, worrying over trifles, lying awake nights with strange mutterings and presentiments, and at times having an uncontrollable temper.

He was a boy of good appearance but now he talked constantly of being old, homely, and ugly looking, and he was so intractable that efforts to reprimand and correct him proved of no avail. This condition became so aggravated that his family despaired of Jack's reason, and so they wrote to Dr. Wickland asking him to concentrate for the child. This was done and a spirit whose actions and expressions were in every way like those the boy had been exhibiting, was attracted to Mrs. Wickland and spoke through her.

"This entity," writes Wickland, "said his name was Charlie Herrmann; he was aware of having died and declared he was a very homely man, with ugly features and a face covered with pock marks. Nobody had cared for him and this fact preyed on his mind.

"Someone had once told him that after death individuals could reincarnate and become whatever they wished to be. Since his only desire was to be good looking, so that others would not shun him, he decided to try and reincarnate.

"As a result, he became entangled in the magnetic aura of a small boy and was unable to free himself."

Finding that he was helplessly imprisoned and incapable of making anyone realize it, Charlie Herrmann had outbursts of temper and "felt like flying to pieces."

"They called me Jack," he said, and he didn't like it. He had been as miserable as the child but could do nothing about it. Through the help he received from the Wicklands he was freed, and very grateful. And Jack became the good and happy boy he used to be.

Dr. Wickland has not only his own testimony and that of his records to verify his statements about reincarnation. He also claims as witnesses for his side songwriter Ella Wheeler Wilcox and Madame Blavatsky, no less!! They purported to speak through Mrs. Wickland and express themselves strongly against reincarnation. Professor C. J. Ducasse speaks of these testimonies in his book *The Belief in a Life After Death* by saying that they are hardly more impressive than Allan Kardec's spirits on the opposite side of the question. For instance, Ducasse points out, what the supposed spirit of Ella Wheeler Wilcox says is that she "would not care to come back . . . would not like to come back to this earth plane again to be a little baby"; that she does "not see why" she should come back! But obviously, Ducasse adds, our likes and dislikes regarding our own future fate never settle the question of what it actually will be.

"The utterances of the purported Blavatsky spirit are

much more categorical," Ducasse continues. " 'Reincarnation is not true,' the spirit says, 'I have tried and tried to come back to be somebody else, but I could not. We cannot reincarnate. We progress, we do not come back.' But although more downright, these statements are no more impressive than those of the Wilcox spirit; for it would be strange indeed that, as those statements would have it, not only the other alleged spirits of former Theosophists quoted in the same chapter, but the spirit of the very foundress of the modern Theosophical movement, should *expect and try to reincarnate just a few years after death,* notwithstanding her own explicit teaching that the interval between incarnations averages from 1000 to 1500 years; notwithstanding her own definite condemnation of the belief of 'the Allan Kardec school . . . in an arbitrary and immediate reincarnation'; and notwithstanding her own teaching that reincarnation takes place not by trying for it, but automatically at the end of many centuries spent in the blissful 'devachan' dream world."

CHAPTER SEVENTEEN

Does Hypnotism Uncover Past Lives?

One of the things known for sure about hypnosis is that some entranced subjects will make every attempt to please the hypnotist, and often carry out what is expected of them. The hypnotist's own beliefs about what he is doing, the tone of his voice, his manner, and his mode or procedure cause the subject to enact faithfully the role thereby handed to him. This is then taken by the hypnotist as evidence confirming the correctness of his original belief. Because this is true, age regression is complicated, and past life regression is problematical, to say the least.

Sidney A. Schneider, a certified hypnotherapist, in his "Report on Hypnotic Age Regression" in *FATE* Magazine, October, 1965, says that hypnotic age regression in other areas is making slow but steady progress, but in psychotherapy it has taken giant strides. From all parts of the U.S. and from all parts of the world, Schneider alleges, clinical use of hypnotic age regression is being reported in scientific papers. One of America's outstanding researchers in the field of hypnosis has stated that in the field of direct, suggestive therapeutics, age regression has been used successfully to abreact traumatic events.

"Just as in most areas of hypnosis, there is no agreement on the nature of regression. Since its discovery in 1887 it has been the subject of constant controversy." The main basis for the controversy over hypnotic age regression stems from the human factor, that is, that differences in personality and investigative experience among hypnotists influence their theories. "They look at age regression subjectively as well as objectively," says Schneider, "and each sees it in a different light. The various differences, however, now have settled into two theories: hypnotic age regression is either a valid phenomenon or it is role playing—acting out a part that the subject believes is expected of him."

While hypnotic age regression can be accomplished with ease in a good subject, it can set off undesirable reactions with which untrained operators may not know how to cope. The hypnotist asks his patient to go back in time to his childhood and recall certain experiences there. Past life regressions ask him to go even further back, to a life earlier than this one, and to tell his memories. They are, quite naturally, undertaken in an attempt to prove whether or not reincarnation is true; and some people maintain that if information apparently is remembered about a past life, this indicates a genuine rebirth. In his book *The Belief in a Life After Death,* Professor C. J. Ducasse gave a thoroughly objective report on *The Search for Bridey Murphy.* He concluded that verifications of the claims about the existence of Bridey Murphy "do not prove that Virginia is a reincarnation of Bridey, nor do they establish a particularly strong case for it." Rather, they constitute fairly strong evidence that, in the hypnotic trances, *paranormal* knowledge of one or another of several possible kinds may manifest itself. Schneider said of this, "It is evident that Professor Ducasse saw beyond the immediate controversy, and by this statement formed a more solid bridge between hypnosis and parapsychology."

One of the first to experiment with hypnotic past-life regression was Colonel Albert de Rochas, who published a book—*Les Vies Successives*—in 1911 about his efforts with a number of people. His report shows the difficulty in evaluating the evidential results of any material purporting to represent a past life. Some of his experiences with an eighteen-year-old girl named Josephine will indicate the problems. De Rochas asked Josephine to think backward in time, past the period of her birth, past the time she was in her mother's womb, and then back to a discarnate period before she was conceived. Then he asked her to give some evidence of a previous life. Josephine began to speak in a gruff man's voice, but would not say a name. Eventually, however, the claim was made that he was Jean-Claude Bourdon, born in 1812 in the village of Champvent, district of Polliat, and that he had died at the age of seventy. Unfortunately, when De Rochas tried later to verify this information, he could find no evidence that a man of that name had lived in that district during that period of time.

De Rochas deepened Josephine's trance and discovered hiding in her girlish memories the personality of a wicked old woman. She said she was Philomene Charpigny, born in 1702. She had married a man named Carteron in 1732 at Chevroux, and her grandfather, Pierre Machon, had lived at Ozan. Families by the names of Charpigny and Carteron were discovered to exist at Ozan and at Chevroux, but there was no positive trace of Philomene herself. Further deepening of Josephine's trance brought out other previous lives as a girl who had died in infancy and a bandit who had robbed and killed.

What then happens to a willing age-regression trance subject when she can think up no more lives to give for her cause? The entranced Josephine solved that one nicely. Ducking her head in humiliation, she admitted that before her bandit incarnation she had been a big ape!

I once saw two lightly entranced young girls age regressed and asked to tell what went on before they came into this life on earth. The one who believed in reincarnation immediately produced some mediaeval history which she claimed to be living in a colorful fashion. The other, who had no opinions about rebirth, was a water fairy or sprite. No matter how she was led to explain it, she could only answer that she was swimming in or flitting about over a rocky pool. She was finally given up as a bad job.

Just the opposite of age regression is age *progression,* in which the subject is taken, by hypnotic suggestion, to a future age. Whether, when predicting their own future, the people are using ESP, role-playing, or mere guesswork, has not been determined. De Rochas progressed his Josephine into the future of her own life; but nothing she predicted came true—at least until the time of De Rochas'

148

death. When he asked her to predict her lives in the future, she said that she would die at the age of seventy and then reincarnate first as a girl, Elsie, who would die when three years old. Then she would come back in 1954 as Marie, the daughter of a man named Edmond Baudin and his wife Rosalie. Her father would run a shoe store at Saint-Germain-du-Mont-d'Or. If such a person as Marie answering that description now lives, will she please stand up—and be counted?

Past life readings have become so commonplace now that almost any medium will give you one, for a sizeable fee. The popularity of Edgar Cayce has started practically a fad. But those who can give their own past life readings when under hypnosis are even luckier, because it costs less, and is much more convincing. Professor Ducasse took shorthand notes of a session held in New York City in February, 1906, when a young woman was regressed during two different experiments by a young physician, Dr. Morris Stark. Ducasse writes in *The Belief in a Life After Death*, that the girl was familiar with the idea of reincarnation and understood that the experiment was to be an attempt to regress her consciousness to a time before the birth or conception of her body. In the record of the two sessions there are hardly any items that would lend themselves to verification by objective facts.

The notes of the two sessions start as follows:

Q: Tell us what you see; where are you now?
A: It is very warm. I am walking out somewhere, the sun is hot, I don't know where I am. It is all growing dark.
Q: The picture will clear up in a minute.
A: The sky is very blue and the sun is very warm, it shines through my sleep. I am walking along the water. The water is very blue and the ships are in the water. I don't know what I am doing here.
Q: What is your name?
A: My name, I don't know. It is very beautiful, not a cloud in the air, there are beautiful trees and plants and a great many people.

Q: How are they dressed?

A: They wear loose, beautiful gowns, not like others I have seen. Their arms are bare, they are talking.

Q: What language? ...

A: Who are you?

Q: I am a friend of yours.

A: The city is on hills, it hurts my eyes. I live over there. It is getting so warm. Had I not better go home? It is by the water.

Q: What is the name of the water?

A: It is some bay, I don't know the name. The city is in the distance. It might be a river, but I think it is too large for a river. There is a building here, all open. There are a great many flowers and inside the floors are marble in blocks, some of them are of different colors.

Q: What year?

A: I don't know, I shall have to go and ask someone.

Now what does all this remind one of? The man named Frank who spoke through Mrs. Wickland—the one who had been possessing the patient named Mrs. Burton at the Institute. So what does that make our hypnotized subject—temporarily possessed by a spirit entity? Or does it make the man named Frank a past life of Mrs. Wickland? Or was it merely some alter-ego of her consciousness, giving forth with the information expected of it, as a kind of role-playing? And if this was so with Frank, how did Mrs. Burton then come to be cured when he left? It is certainly difficult to get any cut and dried answers to anything about this subject. Perhaps that's the challenge of it.

The most famous case of past life regression is, of course, Bridey Murphy, the Irish lass who put the whole United States into a hypnotizzy in 1956. Morey Bernstein, a Colorado businessman who had practiced hypnotism for ten years with hundreds of different persons, decided to attempt to regress someone to a past life. He chose as his subject Virginia Tighe, whom he knew could go into a deep trance easily. Between November 29, 1952, and August 29, 1953, Bernstein made six attempts to have Virginia (whom he called by the pseudonym Ruth Simmons in his book) regress to past lives. She spoke of one brief life as a baby who died. And then came Bridey Murphy—Bridget Kathleen Murphy, if you please. She visited whenever invited after that and gave a good bit of information about Ireland which Virginia Tighe had no normal way of knowing. She said she had been born in Cork in 1798, daughter of a Protestant Cork barrister, Duncan Murphy, and his wife Kathleen. She had a brother named Duncan Blaine Murphy, who had married Aimee Strayne. She had another brother who had died while still a baby. At the age of twenty, Bridey said she was married in a Protestant ceremony to a Catholic, Brian Joseph McCarthy, son of a Cork barrister. Brian and Bridey moved to Belfast where he had attended school and where he eventually taught law at the Queen's University. She had no children and lived until she was sixty-six. No records of any of these facts remain in Ireland. But during her conversations Bridey mentioned the name of two Belfast grocers—Farr's and John Carrigan, and it was verified that these two grocers did have shops there then. She said her address in Cork was "The Meadows," and there is an area there named Mardike Meadows. There was a Queen's University in Ireland. Bridey used certain curious words which were in use in Ireland then, such as "ditched" for "buried," a "linen" to mean a "handkerchief," and "lough" for river or lake. Some supporters of the phenomenon have felt that a girl born and raised in the United States as Virginia was would not be likely to have been acquainted with these terms.

Trying to track down the truth of her statements began the search for Bridey Murphy; and when Bernstein's book *The Search for Bridey Murphy* was published, it seemed that half the newspaper reporters and Irish enthusiasts in the country entered the search, either trying to prove or disprove her existence. The book was an instant hit and a best seller for months. Then there were the newspaper accounts and the magazine arguments and the scientific reports attempting to prove that no such person ever lived and that all the information had come from Virginia

Tighe's subconscious mind. Several people went to Ireland and dug into all the old historical records they could find, and much was made of their results, pro and con, with nothing conclusive being settled.

The one question that didn't receive much argument was the idea that perhaps Bridey was not actually Virginia in a past life, but the actual surviving spirit of Bridey herself speaking. Perhaps Virginia is a medium through whom Bridey spoke about her life on earth, in an effort to prove that she really once lived and that she still lived and was able to communicate. Well, it's one more theory, anyway.

CHAPTER EIGHTEEN

William James, a Message from Beyond

One of America's best-known psychologists, William James (1842–1910), was very active in psychical research during his lifetime. Via automatic writing in recent years, he has maintained that he is still just as interested in what happens on earth concerning investigations leading toward proof of survival. He keeps in constant touch with all that is done regarding parapsychology, mediumship, and all other areas in which there is the possibility of proving that man lives after death. He says that a great many who were similarly interested on earth continue their work and efforts from the spirit planes, for it is vitally important that man know the truth of immortality. So far, the communicant who calls himself William James has done very little in the way of attempting to give evidential material that would tend to prove it is he who is communicating; but he has let his written material speak for itself. You may accept it or reject it as coming from James; you may accept it or reject it as a philosophy of life after death. But I believe you will find the reading of his summary of conditions at least interesting.

The statement, allegedly written by William James, from the spirit world and sent through automatic writing, follows:

"Reincarnation appeals to many people as a logical explanation for many of the problems of life and for the inequalities which so often exist. However, there are theories and there are facts. I would like now to give you the true picture of what happens to you at death. Because all ideas have to have names, the title Evolutionary

Progression has been given to this system of thought.

"Evolutionary Progression maintains that the consciousness of each man born on earth survives death and continues to live forever. He leaves the earth with whatever development he has achieved up to that point. He is not altered in any way by the transition called death. Nothing new has been added, and nothing has been lost except the physical body. The only way that the consciousness, or spirit, may change is by his own efforts. And so it is by his own conscious design that he improves himself. When he begins to realize that his progress depends entirely upon his own efforts, he will start to work on his self-improvement, and then he will begin to advance. His goal is the highest possible spiritual development, which will eventually make him worthy of unity with what is termed God—although I hesitate to use that word because it has so many wrong connotations. Let us rather use the expression Ultimate Perfection. This covers everything of the greatest good, the highest intelligence, and the most universal love. It is the achievement of Ultimate Perfection that is man's goal from the moment he was born on earth, and it must continue always to be his goal.

"As each person advances after death, he does so with awareness of who he is—the same person he was on earth—and where he is going. Granted, it takes a fantastically long time to reach Ultimate Perfection. It could not be otherwise. Granted also that some individuals take a great deal longer than others. That is why it is so important to turn your thoughts in this direction before death. If you die believing that there is nothing more for you, your mind may be closed to the information given you by those helpers who make it a point to pass on the truth to all who come over into spirit planes. If you do not listen, and choose to spend your time wandering about in an unenlightened state, you may waste many eons before you finally decide to set your feet on the proper path.

"Many unintelligent individuals who have been taught that they must reincarnate will attempt to do this, and it leads to that worst of all possible conditions known as possession. I am not now talking of reasoning persons who have evaluated all the good attributes of this philosophy and decided to accept it, not knowing of the bad. They now consider themselves to be reincarnationists, but when they die they will soon listen when told the truth. They will have no problems readjusting. Those of you who read this book have nothing to fear, for you are intelligent seekers after the truth. It is the poor unenlightened Hindus, the low caste individuals who have never thought about any other concepts of life after death, who are the most affected by their wrong beliefs. Not only are they apathetic to life because of their religion, but they frequently attempt to reincarnate after death by possessing another person. Untold harm results.

"Instead of some Essence reincarnated into a number of bodies on earth, which becomes a composite of many men and women before it is through, what actually continues to Ultimate Perfection is the one individual consciousness of each man who is born. This consciousness lived in an earth body to establish his identity, to originate and set his patterns of character and personality. He will change so constantly after he begins his improvement in the spirit world that the original man will hardly be the same in any way; and yet he will always maintain his personal identity, his I-Am, which will never be confused with any other I-Am.

"This person's memories are intact at the moment of death, and he can refer to any of them as he wishes. They do not flood in on him; but they are all available to him when he is ready to review the most intimate details of his life. Ideally, he should do this very soon after his death, and then decide what kind of steps he needs to take to begin to improve himself. As he looks back over his life he will see many areas where he did not live up to his best potential. When he listens to the teachers who are always willing to give him advice about how best to improve himself, he may decide on any one of many programs of self-improvement. He will be ready to start this work at once and to progress as rapidly as possible.

"Unfortunately, many persons who will not accept a new

idea on earth are just as closed-minded after death. However, when they do decide by their own free will to change their situation, they will begin their advancement. It will not be easy to make the character adjustments and reevaluations necessary, but they will have all the help they need from those who are making it their business to assist just such delinquents. When they need advice of any kind, it is available. They will have to work very hard for a very long time, but they will do it by their own conscious efforts, knowing every minute of the way exactly what they are doing and why. In this manner every step is a conscious move toward actual retribution for errors, not a blind reliving of a new life in which new experiences will give the needed lessons."

This is all I have to say about immortality. It's just about all I know on the subject. It makes much less sense if you consider it just as an argument for and against reincarnation; but if you consider it as a discussion of the possibility of life of some kind after death, there might be a few ideas here worth consideration. It is offered, then, for what you can make of it. I have found my belief in immortality to be the most rewarding thing in my life. Perhaps this might start your interest in attempting to find for yourself some philosophy of life after death which might be as helpful to you.

The smash bestseller the whole country is talking about!

Rosemary's Baby

by Ira Levin

SUPPOSE you were a young housewife who moved
into an old and elegant apartment house with
a strange past. SUPPOSE that only after you
became pregnant did you suspect that the
building harbored a group of devil worshippers
who had mastered the art of black magic.
SUPPOSE that this satanic conspiracy set out
to claim not only your husband but your baby.
Well, this is what happened to Rosemary.
Or did it?

DON'T REVEAL THE ENDING

"The climax is an icy shock which no one
will ever quite forget." —*Providence Journal*

Watch for the Paramount movie starring Mia Farrow

A DELL BOOK   95¢

How many of these great science fiction stories have you read?

How many of these Dell Bestsellers have you read?

NICHOLAS AND ALEXANDRA by Robert K. Massie   **$1.25**

THE DOCTOR'S QUICK WEIGHT-LOSS DIET
   by I. Maxwell Stillman and S. Sinclair Baker   **95c**

ROSEMARY'S BABY by Ira Levin   **95c**

THE DEAL by G. William Marshall   **95c**

SEVENTH AVENUE by Norman Bogner   **95c**

THE PRESIDENT'S PLANE IS MISSING
   by Robert J. Serling   **95c**

THE KLANSMAN by William Bradford Huie   **95c**

OUR CROWD by Stephen Birmingham   **$1.25**

THE FIXER by Bernard Malamud   **95c**

GO TO THE WIDOW-MAKER by James Jones   **$1.25**

BASHFUL BILLIONAIRE by Albert B. Gerber   **95c**

THE SHOES OF THE FISHERMAN by Morris L. West   **95c**

THE LAWYERS by Martin Mayer   **$1.25**

MY SILENT WAR by Kim Philby   **95c**

By the author of THE COLLECTOR . . .
John Fowles

the magus

"Fascinating . . . from the black of death and dark arts
to the warm, clear tones of flesh and love and a sunny
Greek island . . . a beautiful, broadloom magic carpet."

—*Detroit News*

"Always—and frighteningly—believable . . . wit and
wisdom interwoven in a complex drama which climaxes with
a Sade-like sexual fantasy that outdoes the master."

—*Playboy*

"A sumptuous firework exhibition . . . brilliant."

—*The New York Times Book Review*

A DELL BOOK 95c

See the dazzling 20th Century-Fox movie starring
Anthony Quinn, Michael Caine, Candice Bergen and Anna Karina.